Marginal
SPACES

Comparative Urban and Community Research

Series Editor, Michael Peter Smith

Marginal
SPACES

COMPARATIVE URBAN AND
COMMUNITY RESEARCH
VOLUME 5

edited by
Michael Peter Smith

Transaction Publishers
New Brunswick (U.S.A.) and London (U.K.)

Second printing 2004

Copyright © 1995 by Transaction Publishers, New Brunswick, New Jersey.

This book is printed on acid-free paper that meets the American National Standard for Permanence of Paper for Printed Library Materials.

Library of Congress Catalog Number: 95-9319
ISSN: 0892-5569
ISBN: 1-56000-812-1
Printed in the United States of America

Library of Congress Cataloging-in-Publication Data

Marginal spaces / edited by Michael Peter Smith.
      p. cm. —(Comparative urban and community research, ISSN 0892-5569 ; v. 5)
   Includes bibliographical references.
   ISBN 1-56000-812-1 (alk. paper)
   1. Community development, Urban—United States—Case Studies.
2. Urban poor—United States—Political activity—Case studies. 3. Marginality, Social—United States—Case studies. 4. Land use, Urban—Political aspects—United States—Case studies. I. Smith, Michael P. II. Series.
HN90.C6M37 1995
307.1'412'0973—dc20
                                         95-9319
                                            CIP

Contents

Acknowledgment

"The Stimulus of a Little Confusion" by Edward W. Soja, which appeared in *After Modernism*, volume 4 of *Comparative Urban and Community Research*, was originally published by the Centrum voor Grootstedelijk Onderzoek (Center for Metropolitan Research) of the University of Amsterdam (1991) as part of its series of "Texts of a Special Lecture." Sponsored by the city of Amsterdam, the CGO supports a program of visiting professors of urban research. Professor Soja was a visiting professor in the spring of 1990 and presented a lecture on "The Changing Relation of City and Suburb in Los Angeles and Amsterdam," from which this more expansive essay derives. Due to an error made in the preparation of camera ready copy for volume 4 this acknowledgment did not appear. Also inadvertently excluded was the following statement by Professor Soja: "Thanks to Leon Deben, Dick van der Vaart, and Jacques van de Ven, for sponsoring my stay in Amsterdam, along with the Department of Social Geography of the University of Amsterdam. Very special thanks also to Pieter Terhorst of the Department of Social Geography, who more than anyone else warmly and informatively shaped my understanding of Amsterdam."

Introduction

The Social Construction of
Marginal Spaces

Michael Peter Smith

> *In reality, social space "incorporates" social*
> *actions, the actions of subjects both individual*
> *and collective, who are born and who die, who*
> *suffer and who act.*
> —Henri Lefebvre, *The Production of Space*

Spatial practices by centers of wealth and power to legitimate their domination and marginalize, exclude, or contain dominated groups, keeping them "in their place," have been extensively studied in urban and community research. The literature on modernist and postmodernist urban development is replete with this theme—the city envisaged as a mechanism of spatial exclusion, surveillance, and social control. A variety of critical theorists from Michel Foucault to Henri Lefebvre have been invoked by contemporary analysts of social space to give resonance and a theoretical gloss to this leitmotif (See, for instance, Soja 1989; see also Davis 1990, chapter 4).The postmodern sensibility has cast interesting light on the way in which language and discourse are used to construct and reproduce spatially distinct centers and margins. Yet once marginal spaces are socially constructed, the "inhabitants" of these spaces have shown a remarkable ability to act in ways that defy the regulatory intentions of their superordinates.

This capacity of marginal groups to refashion spaces of social control into sites of resistance was well recognized by the late Henri Lefebvre. After devoting a large portion of his influential work *The Production of Space* to the theme of capitalist domination of social space, Lefebvre (1991, 362) had this to say about resistance to domination in the everyday spatial practices of marginalized groups:

> Let us now turn our attention to the space of those who are referred to by means of such clumsy and pejorative labels as "users" and "inhabitants." No well defined terms ... have been found to designate these groups. Their marginalization by spatial practices thus extends even to language. The fact is that the most basic demands of "users" (suggesting "underpriviledged") and "inhabitants" (suggesting "marginal") find expression only with great difficulty, whereas the signs of their situation are constantly increasing and often stare us in the face. . . . [T]he space of the everyday activities of users is a concrete one, which is to say subjective. As a space of "subjects" rather than of calculations, as a representational space, it has an origin, and that origin is childhood, with its hardships, its achievements, and its lacks.

Few researchers have taken up the challenge implict in this statement by mapping the subjectivity, and hence the power moves and power plays, embodied in the spatial practices of marginal groups. Put differently, few have studied the social construction of marginal spaces as spaces of resistance "from below." Two theoretically informed observers of the human condition who have done so exceptionally well, Michel de Certeau and James C. Scott, have provided us with useful models for the close study in daily life of what Scott terms "the weapons of the weak." De Certeau's (1984, xxiv) analysis of the practices of everyday life starts from the assumption that in today's fragmented societies the problem of the "subject" is not one of mere dissolution; rather, subjectivity is discernible in the reappropriations of social space made by its actual users. In his words, "[The] ways of reappropriating the product system ... created by consumers, have as their goal a therapeutics for deteriorating social relations and make use of techniques of reemployment in which we can recognize the procedures of everyday practices." He concludes that to understand the workings of power a politics of such ploys should be developed. Scott (1985, 31–38) does precisely this in his richly textured and broadly Gramscian analysis of the forms of everyday resistance by peasants to the claims of superordinates and the state. He moves us well along the path toward an understanding of the politics of a wide variety of socio-spatial ploys—for example, passive noncompliance, subtle sabatoge, and land squatting—whereby the "weak" encroach upon, mitigate, or deny claims upon them made by the "strong."

Each of the contributions to Volume 5 of *Comparative Urban and Community Research* is a case study that combines a structural and historical analysis of the moves of powerful social interests to dominate space with an ethnographically grounded account of the tactics and strategies developed by various marginalized social groups to reappropriate dominated spaces for their own uses. The *Marginal Spaces* embodied in the title of this volume of our series include five sites of dominantion and resistance: a squatters' movement in Ann Arbor, Michigan resisting the adverse consequences of four decades of urban development in that "City of Intellect,"; a homeless encampment in Chicago engaged in "guerrilla architecture," and other moves designed to reconstitute prevailing social constructions of the problem of "homelessness"; an antigentrification movement in the East Village of New York engaged in an ongoing struggle to resist efforts by developers to commodify and market their neighborhood as an "untamed" and hence "exciting" space for luxury condominium development; a Public Housing Council organized by African-American women in New Orleans to resist both the material regulation of their daily lives and the dominant social construction of public housing as a racially gendered space suitable only for "dependent" women and children of color; and a subordinate labor market niche in California agriculture where indigeneous Mixtec peasants from Oaxaca are displacing more traditional mestizo farm workers but also are politically organizing as a transnational grassroots movement pursuing a binational strategy to alleviate their economic, political, and cultural marginality.

In "House People, Not Cars!" Corey Dolgon, Michael Kline, and Laura Dresser combine a historical analysis of urban redevelopment in Ann Arbor with a case study of the resistance practices developed by the Homeless Action Committee, a squatter movement in which they were participant-observers. Their study documents the pivotal role of the University of Michigan in alliance with local political elites, developers, and real estate interests to refashion the image of Ann Arbor into that of a premier regional research center, dubbed by this growth machine a "City of Intellect." Over time, their local office building-oriented development strategy produced gentrification and displacement of traditional black working-class neighborhoods, accelerated postwar economic restructuring trends, led to the closure of single room occupancy hotels (SRO's), drove up rents, and increased homelessness. Their article shows how the restructuring and respatialization of capital at the national and global scales is socially produced by historically specific institutional arrangements, political coalitions, and economic development policies. The authors then discuss the daily practices of a self-consciously "marginal" political action group, the Housing Action Committee (HAC) to block further displacement and change the terms of political discourse on "homelessness" emanating from elite modes of knowledge production that legitimated the growth machine's development trajectory.

The HAC is a local coalition of students, formerly and currently homeless people, and community activists that moved from the practice of providing services to homeless persons (and hence reinscribing the role of homeless people as dysfunctional misfits assigned to them in the dominant discourse) to one of engaging in collective research, analysis, and critique of dominant explanations of economic development. They used research and critique to inform tactics of direct action (e.g., appropriating the public space of a City Counil meeting room; squatting in unoccupied city-owned houses scheduled for demolition to build a publically subsidized downtown parking garage) to highlight the politically shaped pattern of spatial inequality and attendant homelessness, thus moving the discourse beyond the rhetoric of individual pathologies. Dolgon, Kline, and Dresser interpret the tactics and strategies described in their article in Gramscian terms as designed to subvert the prevailing "common sense" of the growth machine and reconstitute the political space of the homelessness debate. These efforts have thus far led not only to the cancellation of the parking structure but to the forging of a wider alliance of interests, including local clergy, university faculty, and environmental organizations, that have coalesced around the need to closely monitor future local land-use issues.

Talmadge Wright's contribution tells the story of another marginal space, a Chicago encampment of plywood huts housing homeless persons, and named "Tranquility City" by one of its members. Tranquility City was a self-constituted squatter settlement on the Near West Side of Chicago that lasted over six months until dismantled by city government authorities, who rendered the social space (and the scale of homelessness) invisible by placing the "inhabitants" of the encampment in Chicago public housing units. Wright uses Melluci's concept of "submerged networks" to explain the emergence of Tranquility City as a rudimentary social network whose members were capable of forging links with both other homeless people and mainstream social institutions to pursue collective objectives. Employing participant observation and extensive ethnographic interviews with the members of the encampment, Wright and a team of student researchers generated a grounded understanding of the creation, development, and demise of this new social movement.

The institutional allies of this homeless network are similar to but even broader than those mobilized in Ann Arbor. They include representatives of local churches, university students and faculty, community activists, artists, radical architects, local volunteers, and even sympathetic commuting suburbanites who had witnessed the "guerrilla architecture" of the plywood encampment. On the one hand, the very breadth of this coalition increased the possibility of internal cleavages. On the other hand, the active and visible participation of homeless persons in a wider campaign for jobs, housing, and food undermined the hegemonic construction of homeless people as disaffiliated and pathological rather than as political actors capable of sustained organizational work who have been marginalized by the scarcity of jobs and affordable housing. In addition to his insightful discussion of the spatial practices of the encampment and the wider coalition, Wright's article offers a useful critique of the inadequacies of the existing "solution" to this social problem—the overnight and transitional housing system in Chicago—particularly the degrading rituals forced upon homeless persons to gain access to these spaces of social control.

The third case study in this volume, by Christopher Mele, offers a detailed account of a decade of struggle involving the state, private developers, and residents of the East Village of New York resisting residential displacement and the commodification of their neighborhood. In this instance, the oppositional coalition is an antigentrification movement, including squatters, former hippies, affordable housing advocates, and community activists, who have used the conversion of a former settlement house into luxury housing units as a catalyst for the creation of a political space for protracted resistance to residential restructuring. Mele's case study fruitfully combines the macroanalytical research tools of urban political economy with a textured ethnography of community level dynamics of displacement. The author's ethnographic vantage point, or "positionality," was established by living for three years in several transitional buildings in the East Village undergoing piecemeal gentrification and displacement. This enabled him to compile a rich account of the versatility of both developers and those resisting their displacement strategies. Mele's interviews with tenants, landlords, developers, and movement activists enabled him to paint an interesting portrait of developers' efforts to market the neighborhood's historical image as a "bohemian" space. Ironically, the "safe zones" of drug dealing in the East Village, while actually highly regulated marginal spaces in New York's underground economy, have provided a backdrop for developers' efforts to market the East Village as an untamed, and thus "exciting" site for luxury housing. Mele characterizes the current political climate in the East Village as one of "contested deadlock."

Low income African-American women living in a public housing project in New Orleans are the subjects of the fourth case study in *Marginal Spaces*. In "Resisting Racially Gendered Space," Alma Young and Jyaphia Christos-Rodgers show that this unlikely setting has become a space of resistance to urban restructuring. The project's Resident Council has become an alternative, self-managed institution, whose members are engaged in a "discourse of resistance" to the dominant institutional culture of urban economic development. Recognizing the power of institutional arrangements to shape everyday life, these women of color have sought to redefine the power relationship between themselves and urban elites by advancing an alternative community-based approach to economic development that challenges the ways in which the corporate city has organized space by means of race, class, and gender hierarchies. In particular they have sought to overturn the prevailing conception of racially gendered space embodied in the official organization of public housing.

Starting from a Foucaultian analysis of discursive practices, Young and Christos-Rodgers show how the official discourse of economic development legitimates segregated "communities of consumption," glorifies elitist spaces, dismantles public space, and stigmatizes the highly regulated spaces where low income people of color are "kept." Young and Christos Rodgers combine ethnographic and institutional analysis to give voice to the impressive multifaceted strategy engaged in by the women on the Resident Council who are acting, thus far successfully, to render social service agencies responsive to their needs; to resist efforts to grab public housing land for private gain; to build alliances for the rehabilitation of the project and the surrounding neighborhood, and to open up some units in their project to working-class families.

In the final contribution to this volume Carol Zabin compares the operation of two competing marginal spaces, the mestizo immigrant social networks from Northern Mexico that traditionally have provided the migrant labor force for California agriculture and the newer transnational social network formed by indigenous peasants from Southern Mexico, particularly Mixtec Indians, who are displacing the former. Zabin's study combines a historical analysis of changing labor relations in California agriculture with a micro-analysis of the current competition for jobs between Mixtecs and mestizos based on interviews with 129 Mixtec field workers from thirty-six villages in Oaxaca. For both groups of farm workers the move to post-Fordist agriculture since the 1970s has meant higher job search costs, uncertain work, dependence on subcontractors to obtain work, cuts in grower-provided housing, and even growing homelessness. Zabin documents the role of growers in taking advantage of the Mixtecs' multiple marginalities and willingness to work for lower wages to drive down harvesting costs. She interprets the ethnic displacement and succession that follows from this grower strategy as the latest stage in a recurrent cycle that has enabled growers to undermine improvements in agricultural wages and working conditions. Nevertheless, she points out that the Mixtecs have organized a grassroots organization that is now operating transnationally and is one of the few viable grassroots organizations in California agriculture today. Others (Nagengast and Kearney 1991; Smith 1994) have detailed the complex and multilayered political and economic strategy now being actively pursued in both Mexico and the United States by this transnational league of Mixtec Indians as they refashion their ethnic identity and use that refashioned identity as a political resource.

References

Davis, Mike (1990). *City of Quartz*. London and New York: Verso.
De Certeau, Michel (1984). *The Practice of Everyday Life*. Berkeley: University of California Press.
Lefebvre, Henri (1991). *The Production of Space*. Oxford: Basil Blackwell.

Nagengast, Carol and Michael Kearney (1990). "Mixtec Ethnicity: Social Identity, Political Consciousness, and Political Activism," *Latin American Research Review,* 25, 2: 61–91.

Scott, James C. (1985). *Weapons of the Weak: Everyday Forms of Peasant Resistance.* New Haven, CT: Yale University Press.

Smith, Michael Peter (1994). "Can You Imagine? Transnational Migration and the Globalization of Grassroots Politics," *Social Text,* 39 (Summer): 15–33.

Soja, Edward W. (1989). *Postmodern Geographies.* London and New York: Verso.

1

"House People, Not Cars!": Economic Development, Political Struggle, and Common Sense in a City of Intellect

Corey Dolgon, Michael Kline, and Laura Dresser[1]

> *For a mass of people to be led to think coherently and in the same coherent fashion about the real present world, is a "philosophical" event far more important and "original" than the discovery by some philosophical "genius" of a truth which remains the property of small groups of intellectuals.*
> —Antonio Gramsci, *Prison Notebooks*

A little before eight-o'clock in the morning on October 6, 1990, the authors of this paper joined other members of the Homeless Action Committee (HAC) in blocking the entrances to a municipal parking lot behind Kline's department store in downtown Ann Arbor. HAC had chosen the parking lot as the site for a noontime rally to "Save Ann Arbor Homes," a reference to the squatted houses (originally opened up by HAC) adjacent to the lot and now threatened with demolition. A successful rally required that we prevent "business as usual" on a valuable parcel of downtown real estate. As it turned out, our blockade of the parking lot led to a confrontation with angry merchants who tried to have us removed by the police. But HAC successfully shut down the lot and the rally proceeded as planned.

Behind the clash between activists and merchants lay a struggle over four decades of development in Ann Arbor. As we will demonstrate, the conflict over the "Kline's lot" is embedded in both a historical analysis of the city's economic growth and political landscape since World War II as well as a specific approach to political activism and intellectual work committed to social struggle. What links activists, developers, and the university, we will argue, is a contest over the meanings and stakes of intellectual work and knowledge production in a city that sells itself as a successful example of how a "postindustrial" urban economy can work. Implicated in such a struggle are several levels of social contestation. Therefore, we begin by looking closely at the political economy of Ann Arbor, detailing the rise of the University of Michigan as an institution committed to scientific research as well as a corporation interested in seeking increased public and private funds to feed its own visions of growth. We continue by examining the creation of a pro-growth regime comprised of local political officials, the city's chamber of commerce, and university administrators whose interests converged in reshaping the city's image as the "Research Center of the Midwest." We will also note evolving tensions within this "ruling bloc" and the strategies employed to solve certain conflicts among business leaders, university officials, and politicians. And we will consider how major economic shifts affected changes in Ann Arbor's built environment causing a double movement of gentrification and displacement that had especially devástating effects on the city's historically black working-class communities.

The second section of this paper investigates how these same forces had a significant impact on the city's economic and political landscape, creating new forms of intense poverty (homelessness) and demanding innovative forms of political organizing. We examine questions of political resistance and mobilization, asking how a political action group, HAC, with few resources and no formal access to power can challenge a community's political and economic elites whose pro-growth ideology has become so embedded in the community's image of itself. In specific, the paper analyzes how HAC creates a complex, historically based, and politically committed common sense that not only counters pro-growth ideology, but challenges the very foundation of Ann Arbor's economic growth—the University of Michigan. By offering a more collective and liberatory sense of intellectual work, HAC undermines the legitimacy of the type of elite knowledge production that is either blatantly linked to the interests of capital and economic growth or naively framed by scholarly claims of neutrality or objectivity.

Building a City of Intellect:
A History of Pro-Growth Development and Displacement

> *Where once there was farmland, new kinds of seeds are planted in some of the hansomest, parklike, industrial acres of the country, and wealth is created out of less than thin air: the operation of the intellect, devoted to research. . . . The economic growth is self-feeding, self-sustaining, and progresses geometrically. [Ann Arbor] is one of the fastest growing U.S. cities, and the growth is highly selective, by choice of the individuals who planned the growth to be a kind most beneficial to the city, an industrial aristocracy of innovators.*
> —Ann Arbor Chamber of Commerce, 1970

Between 1950 and 1990, Ann Arbor (the largest city in Washtenaw County and now the second largest city in Southeastern Michigan after Detroit) almost tripled in size to just over 110,000 people. The growing population was mostly employed in higher education and healthcare-related fields, technological research and development companies, assisting financial and informational service firms, and restaurants, coffee shops, and other businesses involved in producing an increasingly large and profitable gentrified leisure industry.[2] An employment study of Washtenaw County's economic activities demonstrates an overwhelming growth in the total workforce as well as a rise in both the public and private service sector and a decrease in the proportion of total employment comprised by manufacturing jobs. These developments exemplified major trends in U.S. capital: the shift towards a service economy and the related rise of computer technology and informational service industries and a bifurcated labor force characterized by "an increased need for professionals and technicians with special training and expertise in restricted segments of the job market, a reduced number of traditional blue-collar jobs and a greater demand for part-time and low wage skilled service workers to perform very

County Workers	1950	%	1960	%	1970	%	1980	%
Manufacturing	16,000	33	25,000	36.1	33,000	31.5	40,800	28.8
Non-Manufacturing	15,000	31.7	19,000	26.6	27,600	26.4	41,700	29.5
Prof. & Public Services	17,000	35.3	26,700	37.3	44,100	42.1	59,000	41.7
Total	48,000	100%	71,500	100.0	104,700	100.0	141,500	100.0

Source: *Economic Activities in Washtenaw County: An Employment Study 1960–1980*, Washtenaw County Metropolitan Planning Commission, April 1983; 1950 Census Data

routine tasks."[3]

Ann Arbor's successful development as a "specialized service center" was partly due to its already existing "postindustrial" service-based economic structure. As the previous table demonstrates, compared to a much lower national average, over one-third of Washtenaw County's workforce was employed in professional and public services as early as 1950. In Ann Arbor, the percentage of professionals and service-oriented jobs was even higher since the largest manufacturing sites belonging to Ford and General Motors were both located in the neighboring city of Ypsilanti. And most of Ann Arbor's jobs directly or indirectly related to the University of Michigan (one of the country's largest research universities) and the increasing number of R&D firms taking advantage of the school's proximity. Between 1945 and 1990 the U-M grew in enrollment by almost 150 percent to over 32,000 and increased its total revenues from $24 million to $1.6 billion. The largest growth in revenues occurred in the U-M's hospital (35 percent of the 1990 budget), private endowments (almost 14 percent of the 1990 budget as opposed to 3 percent of the 1950 budget), and federally sponsored programs (25 percent of the 1990 budget as opposed to less than 2 percent of the 1950 budget). Much of this federal money came from the Departments of Defense and Energy and went to the College of Engineering and other related programs for the purposes of military research. Numerous university projects established in the immediate postwar period courted both federal and corporate money which in turn fueled the U-M's institutional growth and restructuring that facilitated new production activities for an evolving, knowledge-based, global economy.[4]

Rising from the Ashes: The University of Michigan and the "New Capitalism"

Following World War II, college campuses across the United States experienced rapid growth. Stimulated by the G.I. Bill, an increasingly powerful cultural reliance on a highly credentialled professional-managerial class, and the government's new focus on universities as sites of scientific research, many universities expanded in size and underwent widespread administrative reorganization.[5] At the University of Michigan, most of the organizational changes caused by restructuring occurred in the business and financial offices as a direct result of the school's burgeoning research functions and revenues. Federally funded research for military-related purposes at the college of engineering and national behavior studies rationalizing the rise of a middle-class technocracy conducted by the Institute for Social Research led to the purchase of large plots of land on the city's northside and the construction of tall office buildings in the Central Campus area. The number of administrators and office staff personnel charged with coordinating financial policies, procedures, priorities and transactions increased tenfold. Still, although many research projects were inextricably linked to Cold War-inspired military and cultural knowledge production, the U-M made its most important institutional restructuring efforts around the possibility of attracting private sector research funds.[6]

The drive for corporate research money actually began in 1948 when the U-M Board of Regents established the Michigan Memorial-Phoenix Project as a practical and "living" tribute to U-M men who had died in World War II. The Phoenix Project, an atomic energy research center, would harness the same "resources, brain power, and initiative' that unleashed forces of mass destruction during the war, and convert them into 'peaceful purposes' for promoting the 'world's welfare.'" Predating President Eisenhower's 1953 "Atoms for Peace" program, the Phoenix campaign chairman, Chester Lang (a vice president of General Electric and U-M alumnus) explained that atomic energy research promised the "richest possible peacetime results" if linked to the same "free-enterprise system" that had brought our nation such "great progress in the past." In fact, U-M president, Alexander Ruthven, cautioned that if government maintained complete control over atomic energy research, the result could be a "policy of drifting" where the potential energy source of a "second industrial revolution" would be stymied by political bickering and ideological squabbles.

Thus, unlike the many federally sponsored U-M research programs that began during and immediately after World War II, the Phoenix Project was privately financed, partially by individual contributions from wealthy alumni, but predominantly by large corporate donations raised during a successful $6.5 million fundraising campaign. Eventually, the drive for corporate research funding triggered by the Phoenix Project would represent one of the most important aspects of institutional restructuring at the University of Michigan: the creation of a Development Council.[7]

In 1951, members of the Phoenix Campaign's executive board met to discuss the possibility of making a private fundraising effort permanent. Touting a "New Partnership" and an "Institute for Regional Research" in science and engineering, the U-M was courting major contributions during the Phoenix Campaign by promising that support for academic research could turn big profits for the private sector. In forming a Development Council, Chester Lang, new U-M president, Harlan Hatcher, Phoenix Campaign Director, Alan McCarthy, and a local Ann Arbor financier and U-M alumnus, Earl Cress adopted the Phoenix Project's strategies of inviting major corporate leaders to be on the Council's board of directors as well as tailoring special presentations for specific companies to demonstrate how certain research projects might be applied by each targeted industry. Although the Council claimed that its goal was to survey and meet the "already existing needs" of the university, "from the outset, it [was] contemplated that a Corporation Program would be one of the more important facets of the University's development operation." The list of "obvious" reasons for such an approach included:

1. The somewhat phenomenal success in realizing corporate support, both designated and undesignated, for the Phoenix project.
2. The growing tendency on the part of corporate interests to support higher education within legal and tax limitations.
3. The general encouragement the government and the courts have given in recent months to the authorization of contributions to education.
4. Public announcements of business organizations advocating that colleges and universities deserve the broadest support of business enterprises.
5. The current trend of corporate interests to establish contribution committees and/or corporate foundations to facilitate the allocation of grants for welfare or philanthropic purposes.[8]

Thus, while governmental legislation and court decisions made corporate sponsored research increasingly profitable (companies could make tax-deductable research grants to universities whose work would then be made available for industrial use) the U-M Development Council recognized the imminent explosion of corporate support for universities as sites of scientific research and knowledge production. The Council also realized that the U-M's own potential for growth beyond its "already existing needs" would rest with the institution's ability to take advantage of these corporate prospects. However, as early as 1954, competition with other major research universities was steep for, as one business columnist put it, "latching onto the corporate dollar has become a selling job in a buyer's market."[9]

Although the U-M's College of Engineering had participated in contract research with corporations for over thirty years, the postwar period marked a new phase where engineering faculty and administrators synchronized efforts with the Development Council to solicit increased corporate investments that equated knowledge production with economic growth and economic growth with national progress and the public good. The U-M's Engineering Research Institute 1951 report, which showed an increase in contract research from $100,000 in 1920 to about $250,000 in 1940 to almost $3.5 million in 1951, explained that the wide variety of achievements in pure science shared a common thread: "many . . . have already found technological applications, resulting in new and better work materials and products and in lower production costs; others will eventually lead to more technological advances, which we hope will improve our way of living."[10] In 1952, the Industrial Participation Program (IPP) offered corporations three-year subscriptions to quarterly reports on university scientific and technological research for the sum of $15,000. In 1954, the U-M teamed with Ford Motor Company to build an advanced training center in engineering and business administration on the site of Henry Ford's old mansion in Dearborn, Michigan. Henry Ford, Jr. explained that his company was "especially concerned with the shortage of young scientists needed to maintain our country's progress. . . . [Funding the U-M's Dearborn Center] offers us a practical means for expressing positively our belief in industry's responsibility to education." Meanwhile, another major target of the U-M's Development Council's efforts, General Motors, issued their new policies on funding higher educational programs claiming that "Material progress is the business of industry and intellectual development is the business of our institutions of higher learning. Both are indivisible aspects of our growth as a nation."[11]

Culminating this consensus that economic growth fueled by scientific knowledge production and facilitated by private investment in public institutions of higher education was in the public's interest, the U-M created an Institute for Scientific Research (IST) with a specific branch called the Industrial Development Division (IDD). In 1958, University officials lobbied Michigan state legislators to fund the creation of a research institute whose stated objective was to aid industrial growth. J.A Boyd, the IST's first director, explained that the Institute provided for "the direct state support of industry through a program of science and technology . . . recognizing that not only the economic growth of our state but also our survival as a nation is dependent upon a dynamic program in science and technology." By the late 1950s and early 1960s it had become clear that, although Michigan's industrial growth had benefitted from the postwar boom in the auto industry, these figures had begun to decline. Meanwhile, in accordance with the national defense needs and the growing technological demands of business and industry, the manufacture of electronics, aerospace equipment, chemical and petroleum products were becoming the most important growth industries in the country. In one of the IDD's first major reports comparing the research patterns of Michigan universities with state and national trends, U-M researchers explained that,

> [Since] technological advance is fundamental to economic growth . . . those geographical regions where universities and industry pursue somewhat similar technical interest would offer competitive advantages in the translation of new scientific advance into new products. . . . One of the most likely avenues for achieving the economic growth needed in Michigan during the next decade can be opened by learning how to fully utilize these university resources in a manner compatible with the existing capabilities within Michigan industry and future technological needs.[12]

The most important resource for future growth would be the production of knowledge and by the early 1960s, all the elements of a cutting-edge, scientific research and development institution were in place at the University of Michigan. David Noble has written that the growing partnership between industry and research scientists during the early twentieth century resulted in scientific inquiry's "general shift away from the search for truth and toward utility. . . . Science had indeed been pressed into the service of capital."[13] However, in the first two decades after World War II, not only was the U-M as a site for scientific research "pressed" into the service of capital, but it had restructured to receive an increasing proportion of federal grants and attract large amounts of corporate funding, provided the scientific framework for the ascendency of a new pro-growth ideology, and now stood as the most promising institution for promoting and attracting local economic growth.[14]

Partnership for Growth: Designing the "Research Center of the Midwest"

Although Ann Arbor's population had increased steadily between 1860 and 1940 (averaging about 4,000 new residents every decade) the city almost doubled in size between 1940 and 1965 to over 85,000. Some of this growth can be attributed directly to higher U-M enrollments and expanded U-M operations. But in the immediate postwar years, Ann Arbor itself combined the necessary institutional mechanisms, ideological frameworks, and pro-growth coalitions to create what Clark Kerr would describe in 1964 as a "City of Intellect" where "clustering universities . . . have clustering around them scientifically oriented industrial and government enterprises."[15] Both the Ann Arbor City Council and the Ann Arbor Chamber of Commerce had passed resolutions in support of the Michigan Memorial-Phoenix Project. Stating that the Project represented "American free-enterprise in one of its most significant manifestations," the city's Chamber of Commerce recognized that "members of this community, particularly of its commerce and industry, will be the first to benefit from the work carried on at the center . . . " and resolved to "do everything in its power to forward the aims and purposes of the Michigan Memorial Phoenix Project." Over the next fifteen years, Ann Arbor's City Council, Planning Commission and Chamber of Commerce would link up with U-M officials in a campaign to make Ann Arbor the "Research Center of the Midwest."

Throughout the late 1940s and early 1950s, Ann Arbor's City Planning Commission declared that land annexation was needed "for the normal growth and expansion of the city." Echoing the *Ann Arbor News* claims that the city had grown "too big for its breeches," the

Commission advised the City Council to annex land at a rapid pace. Part of the commission's and the council's anxiety derived from a growing postwar housing crisis caused by returning veterans and the related rise in U-M student enrollments from 12,000 in 1945 to 21,000 in 1948. Some temporary housing was established by relaxing standards for the leasing of rooms and apartments and by converting Ypsilanti's Willow Run Bomber Plant worker-housing facilities to U-M married student housing. Still, more land was needed to build single family, owner-occupied housing—the type of housing that the Planning Commission argued, "guarantee[s] good citizenship." The commission also feared that inadequate housing might drive people outside city limits and increase suburbanization, a process that would divert state-collected taxes from the city and make "balancing the budget" more difficult.[16]

As early as 1950, however, the commission made it clear that the need for annexation was inextricably linked to local interests in economic growth. Although single family homes create good citizens, more apartments were needed to facilitate the U-M's growth. According to the commission, increased residential development would be necessary to attract faculty and administrators, as well as create an enticing environment for new businesses and industries. Similarly, the Washtenaw County Planning Commission conducted an industrial survey in 1949 to "act as a guide to industrial management seeking new plant locations." Both commissions were headed by important local business figures (Ann Arbor's by John Swisher—realtor, and Washtenaw's by Earl Cress, banker) and comprised mostly of local developers, bankers, politicians, and U-M administrators. Thus, although the goals of planning local expansion efforts arose from issues of "normal growth," "normal" was generally defined by the very specific interests of local business people and university administrators, while "growth" itself was proclaimed as both "natural" and inherently in the public's interest.[17]

Given this context, the promise of successful mayoral candidate, William Brown, to "run the city like a business" seemed both appropriate and necessary. During his twelve-year tenure (1945–1957), Brown engineered numerous land acquisitions, doubling the size of Ann Arbor from 3,900 to 7,885 square acres. Two of the largest annexations were the entire city of East Ann Arbor (655 sq. acres) and a huge chunk of the U-M's newly acquired North Campus (300 sq. acres).

Brown also established a landmark agreement with the U-M that mandated that the University pay lump sums for fire and police services, and $5,000 for utilities per each new building erected. While the contract allowed the city to recoup certain losses created by the University's large, tax-exempt landholdings, it also facilitated U-M growth by committing city services and utilities to future campus development. This agreement laid the groundwork for the most significant examples of a city-University partnership: the courtship of Bendix Aviation Corporation and Parke Davis and Company to Ann Arbor, and the construction of the Greater Ann Arbor Research Park.[18]

On April 12th and May 14th of 1956, Brown and City Administrator Guy Larcolm met with officials from the U-M and Parke Davis to discuss the possibility of the Detroit-based pharmaceutical company locating a medical research laboratory in Ann Arbor. For almost a decade, the U-M had been developing closer relations with Parke Davis through both the Phoenix Project research and various other contracts and scholarship grants. Parke Davis had also participated in the Engineering Research Institute and other U-M Development Council projects. According to a company spokesman, these relationships to research facilities, programs, projects, and personnel "strongly attracted" Parke Davis to Ann Arbor.[19] The plan designed by city officials, U-M administrators, and the company required the city to annex the property, zone it appropriately, and facilitate the necessary linkage to services and utilities. Brown describes the deal to the City Council in the following letter:

> The addition of the Parke Davis research center would be of tremendous value to the City of Ann Arbor. . . . In addition to having the added taxes, we would have the fine people that Parke Davis & Company would bring to Ann Arbor as residents of our City. It is exactly this kind of development we want, and I am sure that the Council will feel that we should do everything possible to obtain this fine institution.[20]

Later that summer, John Swisher wrote to Brown that Bendix Company officials had met with both himself and U-M chief financial officer, William Pierpont about the possibilities of moving their research headquarters to Ann Arbor. According to Swisher, "their requirements are nearly identical with Parke Davis. . . . The 28th of this month they are having talks with the University. I assured them we would cooperate 100%." And they did. By 1959, both Parke Davis and Bendix had built research facilites on the city's northeast side, close to the U-M's burgeoning engineering complex and completely linked to Ann Arbor's expanding city services.[21]

These industries were also linked to Ann Arbor's own evolving image of itself as a growing urban area whose economic development hinged on the rise of scientific research. City administrator, Guy Larcolm, claimed that Parke Davis and Bendix were the "first two industrial developments of any size in Ann Arbor in many years and are possibly the forerunner of additional research-type plants."[22] City officials, like the U-M Development Council, recognized that corporations and government were making more money available for research and development work and the drive for innovation in science and engineering could be the foundation for a major economic transformation. Ann Arbor's successful courtship of Bendix and Parke Davis inspired the city's Chamber of Commerce to coordinate a campaign that might attract more R&D firms to the city. In 1958, the Chamber's Economic Development Committee created the campaign slogan of Ann Arbor as the "Research Center of the Midwest," and initiated a plan to promote both the city's physical and cultural location as ideal for "the right type" of industries. The pinnacle of this effort was the Greater Ann Arbor Research Park (GAARP).[23]

A brainchild of the Chamber of Commerce Economic Development Committee, the GAARP represented the first large-scale coordinated effort among Ann Arbor's business community, U-M administration, and city officials. The committee itself was comprised of Mayor Cecil Creal, City Administrator Larcolm, U-M Engineering College Dean, Steven Attwood, U-M administrator, John McKevitt, U-M Alumni Representative, Gilbert Bursley, and representatives from area banks, realtors, and the two newest R&D facilities—Bendix and Parke Davis. Thomas Dickinson, one of the Committee's co-chairs, the chamber director, and also an officer for the Ann Arbor Trust Company, had cut his organizational teeth as the assistant director for the U-M's Development Council. In his "Recipe For A Research Park," written for *Michigan Business Review*, Dickinson explained that Ann Arbor had always been "known" because of the University of Michigan's "international reputation." The city's expanding "directory of research and development facilities" followed naturally the growing University which "sustains and nourishes the type of highly diversified basic and applied research program on which commerce and industry thrive." With more and more cities, states, and geographic regions scrambling to attract these new industries and their "resultant economic benefits," Dickinson concluded that, GAARP represented a "refreshing and shining example of what an individual community can do to help itself and its neighbors—employing individual and group initiative towards a common objective."[24]

By the early 1960s, the Chamber of Commerce had recognized the same kind of economic trends that had inspired the U-M to establish a Development Council and court increased corporate research money. The seeds of what Manuel Castells has called a "new socio-economic organization of capitalism" were being planted and sown around the globe and major universities evolved as both sites of research and development as well as stimuli for local growth involving knowledge-based production.[25] A coalition of U-M administrators, city officials, and local businessmen responded to these shifting forces and organized as the Chamber of Commerce's Economic Development Committee. This group formed a powerful pro-growth coalition that not only effectively refashioned Ann Arbor's economic development strategies, but created a campaign whose image of the city as "the Research Center of the Midwest" became the focal point of a pro-growth ideology that equated attracting the "right type" of industries with the public good. Although development projects did not go unchallenged, few groups could compete with the organization and resources of the Chamber and its two imposing partners: the University and the local government. When Guy Larcolm asked the Chamber of Commerce in 1965 how one makes a "lovely college town into a great university city," he concluded that the city's plans could not be what everyone wanted, but would be ideally "a realistic projection of a composite community sentiment." The Chamber responded by issuing a challenge to their membership to become more physically and vocally active, "to demonstrate that the business community stands together for 'what's best for Ann Arbor.'"[26]

Development and Displacement in the Postindustrial Downtown

Ann Arbor's transformation from a small university town into a booming center of "postindustrial" economic production met with various levels of resistance throughout the 1960s, 1970s, and 1980s. When the Chamber of Commerce called its membership to action in 1966, they did so in response to what they perceived as local government's overemphasis on "esthetic and sociological" problems. Although the Chamber characterized most zoning battles, sign ordinances, building restrictions and other growth-related constraints as aesthetic issues, protests arose from a variety of organizations and interests. Some challenges came from the U-M student-based radicalism of the Ann Arbor Tenants Union and the Human Rights Party, while others advanced the status concerns of upper middle-class homeowners, in an example of what Mike Davis calls "homestead exclusivism."[27]

Fragments also formed within the business community itself, generally around struggles over downtown versus peripheral growth-oriented projects. These arguments climaxed over the Briarwood Mall project. Built in 1968–69 on the Southeastern corner of the city, the Mall brought together downtown merchants fearful of central business district decay with environmentalists concerned about threatened wetland areas, and property owners organizations worried about highway expansion and increased taxes. The coalition failed to stop the project and quickly dissipated. However, the volatile split in pro-growth interests—downtown versus periphery—would continue over the next two decades and eventually demand special attention from a changing pro-growth coalition.[28]

Meanwhile, what the Chamber termed "sociological" problems were, in fact, "race relations" issues and would appear even more pertinent as the effects of various pro-growth strategies became evident throughout the late 1960s and 1970s. In the early 1960s, an increasingly militant Ann Arbor chapter of the NAACP pressed for a strong fair housing ordinance and the city's Human Relations Commission (a result of the city's first civil rights struggle in the mid-1950s) pressured the *Ann Arbor News* to remove racially discriminatory qualifications from their employment and housing classified ads. The HRC also publicly condemned local businesses that mistreated African American customers, often leading to informal boycotts of certain establishments. Yet a 1964 Employment Survey by the HRC demonstrated that life for blacks in Ann Arbor had not improved much since their first survey in 1956. Jobs, neighborhoods, and schools remained segregated, not by written laws but by a combination of "traditional" prejudices and practices. In a meeting with local real estate agents called by HRC, one realtor described his agency's discriminatory policies by explaining that the realtors weren't purposely creating segregation, they only "represented public opinion" and acted out of an "economic necessity." In response, Emma Wheeler, NAACP President, claimed it was "atrocious" that such heavy discrimination and bigotry against blacks still existed in Ann Arbor, a city of such "higher learning" that it refers to itself as the "research center of the midwest."[29]

Wheeler's husband, Dr. Albert Wheeler, was a former NAACP president and by the early 1970s, had become a powerful civil rights leader in Ann Arbor's black community. As an executive board member of the local Model Cities Program, as a rising figure in the city's Democratic party, and as mayor from 1975 to 1978, he kept a close eye on the effects that economic development policies had on African Americans in Ann Arbor. In particular, Wheeler was concerned with the rapid displacement of residents from the traditionally black, North Central area communities resulting from increasing office development and gentrification projects. On the other hand, Wheeler's 1977 opponent and eventual successor, Republican Louis Belcher, ran a campaign reminiscent of William Brown in 1945. Instead of promising to "*run* the city like a business," though, Belcher proposed shifting much of city government's focus over to meeting business interests. His vision of government's responsibility, aside from fulfilling basic neighborhood services like trash removal and road repair, revolved around encouraging enough economic development so that both downtown and peripheral interests could profit. Their mayoral race in 1977 marked an important crossroads for the city's development policies as Wheeler tried to address the effects that postwar growth took on the city's black and white working class while Belcher attempted to deal with a central business district merchant class fearful of peripheral development.

From 1860 to 1960, Ann Arbor's African American community remained economically and geographically stable. Don Deskins' comprehensive study of black settlements in the city showed five well-defined sections (all located on the Northside) where over 85 percent of Ann Arbor's black population lived. Most African American families owned homes and small parcels of land that they had purchased from previous black settlers through familial connections or friendships. Although a relatively small portion of the entire population (4.7 percent in 1960), blacks comprised a crucial aspect of the city's postwar economic growth. According to Deskins, just over 50 percent of Ann Arbor's African Americans were employed in professional and related services in 1960, "with a greater number being engaged in the related services (practical nurses, nurses aids, hospital attendants, orderlies, cooks, kitchen helpers, etc.) at the hospitals." The HRC Survey of 1956 found similar evidence that blacks formed an important core of Ann Arbor's low-wage, service sector work force. The University of Michigan and the existence of two nearby hospitals (the U-M's and St. Joseph's) had historically provided these positions and the massive postwar growth in these institutions created an even greater need for low-wage service jobs. By 1960, the city's black population had reached 3,176; by 1970 it had doubled to 6,683 and By 1980 it grew to over 10,000. In 1960, the unemployment rate for blacks in Ann Arbor was 7.9 percent—the lowest in the state, while the yearly median family income among nonwhites was the highest in the state at over $5,500. Although these statistics were still much worse for blacks than whites (unemployment was only 2.9 percent for whites and their median family income was over $7500), by 1960, Ann Arbor's African American neighborhoods had the necessary historical and geographical roots, stable economic base, and informal networks of solidarity (churches, social groups, etc.) to comprise a strong sense of community identity, culture, and material stability.[30]

However, one of the most important statistics from the Deskins study is that, although blacks made up only 5 percent of the homeowners in Ann Arbor, their houses made up 30.6 percent of the city's dilapidated housing stock and almost 25 percent of the deteriorating housing stock. A 1960 "Population and Housing" study by the Ann Arbor City Planning Commission showed that Census Tracts 7 and 8, which contained all five African American districts cited by Deskins, had the lowest property values in the city. From 1949 to 1959, Ann Arbor's total population increased 16,000 (33 percent), but from 1960 to 1970 the increase was over 30,000 (almost 50 percent). As the study predicted, and as the Planning Commission's 1963 Guide to Action for the downtown area corroborated, the housing demand would continue to increase in the Central Business District and its connected areas close to the University and burgeoning medical complexes that included much of the North Central Area. During this period, early stages of gentrification began in the traditionally black neighborhoods. Young white professional families bought relatively cheap houses and fixed them up. Meanwhile, in an attempt to ward off large-scale development projects, a fledgling group of black middle-class property owners forged an alliance with their new white neighbors and formed the

North Central Property Owners Association (NCPOA). While their membership helped to maintain a certain neighborhood integrity, the NCPOA's interests rested mostly in improving property values and "community appearances." The group strongly supported Code Enforcement Improvements in the late 1960s that actually sped up the pace of gentrification as many black and other low-income homeowners in the area couldn't afford to keep their homes up to code. With property values and, consequently, property taxes rising, some families were forced out while others were able to sell their homes for a reasonable profit. However, it was unlikely they would be able to find comparable new homes in Ann Arbor's booming housing market. Most either moved to newly built townhouse cooperatives or public housing units on the outskirts of the city, or relocated in the neighboring city of Ypsilanti and its surrounding areas.[31]

This process of gentrification and displacement intensified in the 1970s as not only housing demand remained high, but developers and city officials turned their attention to the necessity of revitalizing the downtown CBD. The City Council and Chamber of Commerce commissioned a joint Central Area Policy Plan to study the CBD, partially in response to Briarwood, but mostly in recognition that (1) property values were still relatively low in the northern segment of the CBD (the Northside communities) and (2) that the booming high-tech businesses on the city's fringes, the growing affluence of the city's burgeoning professional class, and the expansion of city and county governmental services traditionally located in Ann Arbor's CBD all promised an expanding market for office space and related development projects. Although the plan recognized "people" as a "key ingredient" for downtown vitality and suggested a strong "residential" component to CBD strategies, most of the recommendations discussed parking improvements, expanding government services, entertainment spots (restaurants and hotels), and tertiary retail services. The report concluded that the downtown area should not "compete with Briarwood," but should "maintain and strengthen [itself] as the place within the city which serves as a community focus and which depicts Ann Arbor's community identity, while at the same time continuing to serve the *normal* needs of central area residents for goods and services."[32]

For much of Ann Arbor's black community, it was too late to worry about "normal needs." University hospital expansion, parking lots, and expensive apartment buildings catering to medical students and other middle-income hospital employees had destroyed most of the housing on Fuller Road, Glen and Catherine Streets, as well as on Wall St. and Maiden Lane—two of the five traditionally black districts cited by Deskins. Although Ann Arbor's Model Cities program (1969–1974) tried to intervene in various development projects that threatened the remaining neighborhoods, internal fragmentation and external pressures from city council neutralized their abilities. Throughout the 1970s, realtors, developers, and city officials went through the Northside black neighborhoods (sometimes door-to-door) convincing homeowners to sell. When Al Wheeler became mayor in 1975, he commissioned a "Northside Character Study" from the Ann Arbor Planning Department to intervene in the gentrification and commercialization process. The study elicited a wide variety of perspectives and interests in compiling a report on the area's major issues. But, as one resident put it: "The character of the neighborhood has already changed—old houses have been divided for student rentals; some have been replaced by modern brick apartments that are scattered throughout the area. . . . Businesses are moving out from the center of the city and more houses are going to commercial uses." The study's most interesting observation, though, was that many Ann Arbor residents had comments which "seemed to be in direct conflict with one another." The report concluded that, "these opposing opinions could be seen in part as representing different interest groups living or working in the area . . . business people, developers, homeowners, renters, community professionals, young, old, black, white, people who were working to protect what they had and others who were actively capitalizing on an investment." And it was these investment interests that Wheeler's 1977–78 opponent, Lou Belcher represented.[33]

Belcher's occupational resume reads like a tribute to the rise of a "postindustrial" economy. After brief stints at Ford Motor Co. and National Cash Register, Belcher worked for Veda Inc., an Ann Arbor-based pioneer in high technology. Veda participated in various aspects of almost all major American missile projects including Nike, Sparrow, Genie, Eagle, Phoenix, Jupiter, Thor, Polaris, and Saturn weapons systems. At Veda, Belcher began a partnership with two colleagues and the trio eventually left Veda to form First of Ann Arbor Co., whose specialty involved evaluating the design, performance, and testing methods of combat aircraft and the weapons they carry. In the early 1980s, Belcher bought out Third Party Services, a biotechnology leasing company that also invested in various city development projects. Like local businessman/politician William Brown before him, Belcher campaigned for mayor as a friend to merchants, developers, realtors, and other parties interested in furthering government's pro-growth role. In particular, Belcher championed the idea of creating a Downtown Development Authority (DDA). Michigan's State Legislature had passed a law in 1975 permitting municipalities to "correct and prevent deterioration in business districts" by establishing development authorities with the power to design plans for promoting economic growth, and the ability to collect taxes, issue bonds, and use tax increment financing to complete their plans. When Belcher defeated Wheeler in 1978, he paved the way for increased development projects in the downtown by coordinating the construction of the DDA and by helping to rezone areas for commercial use.

Perhaps the most dramatic example of Belcher's direct involvement in a development project that resulted in displacement was the struggle over the fate of the Downtown Club, a single-room occupancy (SRO) boardinghouse in the city's downtown district. Between 1980 and 1982, two other nearby SROs had closed, one converted into a parking lot and the other into apartments, thus causing the loss of dozens of low-income housing alternatives. Belcher and two associates sought to convert the Downtown Club into commercial office space which would have resulted in the loss of another seventy rooms. The Club's owner sold the building to Belcher after utilities had been shut off and residents forced into the streets. This time, however, former residents and community activists fought to keep the building open as low-income housing and eventually struck a bargain with Belcher to delay any rennovations. After failing to reach a permanent agreement, though, Belcher and associates used over half a million dollars in federal funding—obtained by "donating" the building's ornate entry hall to the Ann Arbor Historical Society—and rennovated the space for office use. By the time Belcher left office in the mid 1980s, millions of dollars had been invested in building downtown office space and upscale retail establishments, particularly restaurants and taverns catering to an increasingly affluent professional-managerial class.

Although the process of development and displacement in Ann Arbor reflects a restructuring and respatialization of capital on a global and national level, this first section has sought to explain how specific local institutions, pro-growth coalitions, and economic development policies have harnessed these large-scale transformations to affect local growth. Since World War II, the University of Michigan has occupied an increasingly significant position in regard to fulfilling private interests in knowledge production, and has itself become a corporation whose growth interests are fueled by attracting large amounts of public and private capital for research programs, land acquisitions, and building projects, more staff and more prestige. Local officials and university administrators teamed with the pro-growth strategies of the city's Chamber of Commerce to facilitate both U-M expansion plans as well as local developers' interests in Ann Arbor's own economic growth. Yet, as the city attracted high-tech firms and an increased number of highly paid young professionals and technocrats, the resulting respatialization of capital investment, shifts in housing preferences and consumer tastes, and the burgeoning demand for downtown office and retail space started a process of gentrification that devastated the traditionally black working-class neighborhoods overlapping the downtown area. The displacement of low-income and working-class people from this section of Ann Arbor is a direct result of international economic transformations, national and state-wide legislation, and the workings of a local pro-growth coalition which included the main "driving force" in the city's economy, the University of Michigan. However, these transformations have also inspired new forms of resistance that have recently organized to challenge the city's pro-growth hegemony and the dual process of development and displacement their ideology and practices represent.

Challenging the "New Economy":
Political Resistance in the Post-Industrial City

> First of all, therefore, [a philosophy of praxis]
> must be a criticism of "common sense," being
> itself initially, however, within "common
> sense" in order to demonstrate that "every-
> one" is a philosopher and that it is not a
> question of introducing from scratch a
> scientific form of thought into everyone's
> individual life, but of renovating and making
> "critical" an already existing activity.
> —Antonio Gramsci, *Prison Notebooks*

The crisis of "homelesness" first appeared in the national news media in late 1982. Postwar urban renewal projects displaced many working-class and low-income neighborhoods. Meanwhile, as Hopper et al. explain, the effects of "deindustrialization" not only meant the relocation of "smokestack industries" and the loss of manufacturing jobs, but also the rise of an affluent professional class and the "refurbishing" of urban environments. They conclude, "as cities are transformed from nodes of industry into commercial centers of financial and real estate transactions, information trading, and the allied professional and technical support services they require, a new class of employees and tenants has cropped up."[34]

The subsequent forces of revitalization and gentrification resulted in upscale, downtown development projects, and caused increased pressure to "clean up" central business districts to facilitate a more "profitable" climates. The razing or conversion of low-income housing (including SROs and other "eyesores") intensified the rate of displacement, especially among recently deinstitutionalized mental health consumers who remain most vulnerable to changing housing patterns. The depletion of affordable shelter and the rise of people in need of inexpensive housing converged with Reagan era policies of slashing budget authority and tax expenditures for low-income housing programs. Thus, although mainstream conceptions, media portrayals, and policy decisions regarding homeless people continue to be framed by the language of individual failure and pathological behavior, the rise of homelessness in the 1980s and 1990s is inextricably linked to the political, economic, and cultural shifts in postwar society.[35]

In Ann Arbor, many of these forces combined to cause a new kind of housing crisis in Ann Arbor. Although the immediate postwar period had witnessed a city-wide housing shortage caused by massive university growth and returning veterans taking advantage of the G.I. Bill at the U-M, the economic and social forces of the "new economy" resulted in an increasing shortage of affordable housing. During the 1980s, as rents skyrocketed and gentrification continued, Ann Arbor's low-income housing crisis worsened and homelessness grew. Although city officials claimed that most homeless people in the city came from elsewhere to take advantage of the city's liberal policies and social service networks, a survey taken in 1983 at St. Andrews Church (the city's only night shelter) found that over half had lived in Ann Arbor for more than a year and an even larger percentage were residents of the county. To counter city government's lack of action in addressing the increasing problem of homelessness, a group of community activists, students, and downtown residents (some of them formerly or currently homeless) formed the Homeless Action Committee (HAC) in 1987. Committed to direct-action tactics, HAC demanded and won the city's commitment to lease a space where the Shelter Association could provide daytime counseling and job services for homeless people. But HACs work over the next five years transcended acheiving immediate service provision for those affected by local and large-scale economic changes and aimed at both developing an analysis and advocating for policies that comprehended the full range of economic, social, and political dynamics at the root of homelessness. [36]

What makes HAC's political work unique, we feel, is the group's practice of *collective* research and analysis, its ability to *revise* its analysis in the light of lessons learned through political struggles, its sustained and sophisticated *critique* of dominant explanations of economic development, and its commitment to direct *action*. Together, these four dimensions of political practice comprise what we call HAC's oppositional common sense, through which the group has articulated and publicized an explanation of homelessness that emphasizes political decisions about development instead of individual failures and pathologies, and challenges both local politicians as well as various institutions involved in policymaking.[37]

Putting Housing on the Agenda

Soon after HAC secured a space for the day shelter, and in the midst of claims from city council members that the city *wanted* to do something about homelessness but simply had no resources for low-income housing, the DDA announced its plan to spend nine million dollars to build a parking structure in downtown Ann Arbor. HAC first directed public attention to the Kline's lot project (named for the proposed location of the structure behind Kline's department store) by organizing pickets in front of the store and in front of the lot. Next, HAC members took over the seats of city council members to hold a "People's Council." As council members scrambled to shut off community access cable television cameras, the People's Council publicized city priorities that put parking ahead of housing and passed people's resolutions recognizing the right of all Ann Arbor residents to affordable housing and the city's obligation to address the problem of homelessness by making a commitment to building low-income housing. HAC took the struggle over the Kline's lot to a new level in late 1989 and early 1990 when the group squatted two city-owned and unoccupied houses slated to be demolished to make way for the parking structure. The squatted houses, maintained as housing for homeless men and women for more than a year before one was destroyed and the other relocated, "put a human face on homelessness" (in the words of one HAC member) and kept downtown development at the center of the debate about housing.[38]

Ultimately, HAC's work led to the cancellation of the planned parking structure. Numerous speeches to the city council, a rally in the parking lot and the collection of more than five thousand petition signatures in an effort to place the proposed structure on a ballot kept the lot in the public eye until the mayoral election of 1991, when the incumbent mayor declared that the upcoming vote should serve as a referendum on the parking structure. His defeat was quickly followed by the new mayor's decision to cancel plans for the structure. This victory convinced HAC activists that significant political mileage could be gained by focusing on the connections between downtown development and homelessness. The group's next project, a walking tour of downtown Ann Arbor that pointed out the specific sites where low-income housing had been destroyed to make way for development projects sponsored by the city and benefitting merchants and developers, elaborated HAC's analysis of development and displacement, and led to direct action campaigns that once again focused public attention on government priorities and the historical roots of the city's housing crisis. This brief summary of HAC activism makes clear the reciprocal relationship between action and analysis within the group. HAC has made a conscious decision to employ direct action tactics, to analyze the successes and failures of individual actions, and to integrate the analysis into future plans for action. Below, we will examine how this method guided the group's transition from the successful Kline's lot campaign to the attempt to publicize and act upon a more sophisticated analysis of economic development.

The Struggle Over Downtown Development

In the months leading up to the October 1990 rally in the Kline's lot, the squatted houses had begun to fall out of the public eye, partly because HAC's activity had shifted to other housing issues. Meanwhile, Republicans on the city council grew increasingly hostile toward the squatting campaign; HAC knew that the Republican majority on council wanted to see the squatted houses emptied before the April, 1991 city election. Recognizing the threat of eviction and demolition, HAC felt that hostile members of city council would be far less likely to force homeless squatters into the streets during the winter if public awareness of the squatting campaign remained high. Thus, in September, HAC decided to concentrate on keeping the Kline's lot in the public eye throughout the coming months. The first step in this strategy was the decision to hold a rally to "Save Ann Arbor Homes."

The theme of the rally explicitly connected homelessness to economic development, appealing for community support to fight off developers and their bulldozers. Having already succeeded in putting low-income housing and homelessness on the political agenda, HAC took on the task of mobilizing an alliance of community groups around broader issues of economic development. Accordingly, HAC invited representatives from Unity (a local public housing tenants' organization), organizers from the Ann Arbor Tenants' Union, various student organizations, and various local clergy, to speak about the need for organized community opposition to the power of landlords, banks, and developers. Furthermore, the decision to hold the rally in the parking lot adjacent to the squatted houses almost guaranteed a confrontation with downtown merchants who claimed they relied upon the availability of parking to compete with shopping malls on the periphery of the city. HAC's common sense, however, understood that building a coalition to fight against the forces behind downtown development would mean struggling against merchants, developers, and elected officials.[39]

On the morning of the rally, an early presence enabled HAC to block the two entrances to the lot. When an angry merchant attempted to move a barricade, proclaiming his "constitutional right to park," HAC members and supporters immediately sat down in front of the car. Police arrived promptly, but on orders from city hall did not arrest those blocking the driveway. Quick thinking and experience with direct action tactics had ensured HAC's use of the lot for the rest of the day. The rally, including speakers, music, and the construction of a symbolic house, solidified both HAC's own membership (including several reticent members who spoke in public for the first time) and its ties to other progressive community groups who participated in the event.

After the rally, HAC discussed what had been successful and what had not, what the event had achieved and altered. Members were pleased with the large turnout but disappointed that the crowd was predominantly students. To HAC, city hall's decision not to break up the occupation of the lot despite merchants' complaints meant that the city council recognized HAC's power in the community. Yet HAC failed to fully anticipate and prepare for the conflict with angry and surprisingly violent merchants. HAC members were also disturbed by what they saw as distorted media portrayal of the action in the next day's *Ann Arbor News*. The *News* reported on the rally as an aggravation to merchants and framed the conflict between activists and merchants as simply a contest over rights: the rights to park and to profit weighed against the right to protest. HAC thus realized that it would have to get its analysis of homelessness and development out to the public on its own.

The city's decision six weeks later to bulldoze one of the squatted homes provided HAC's next opportunity to mobilize and demonstrate. At the city council meeting following the destruction of "Day One" (HAC's name for the first house the group squatted) HAC members and supporters held a vigil in council chambers to commemorate the house "killed by council." The group criticized the city council's Orwellian use of language that equated housing destruction with downtown development, and interrupted the proceedings repeatedly chanting "house people, not cars!"

As winter progressed, the mayor and council stepped up their threats to evict the residents of the remaining squatted house. While approaching friendly members of council about a way to postpone eviction and possibly save the house through relocation, HAC debated internally the wisdom of working to get the parking structure on a referendum ballot. State legislation permitted citizens to call for a referendum on the issuing of bonds for DDA projects by collecting enough petitions within forty-five days of the vote to initiate the sale. HAC's decision to canvass for petition signatures in the month before the city elections, together with Mayor Jernigan's pronouncement that the mayoral race should be a referendum on the parking structure, not only made the Kline's lot a central campaign issue, but also put the eviction process on hold until after the election. Jernigan's defeat paved the way for his successor, Liz Brater, to cancel the structure and agree to move the remaining squatted house and an adjacent house (never a target of the squatting campaign because it was already occupied) across the street where they would be renovated and reopened as low-income housing.

All along, HAC had understood the proposed parking structure as a dramatic example of Ann Arbor's own brand of gentrification: commercial development that displaced low-income residents from the downtown. After the defeat of the parking structure, the group wrestled with the question of where to direct its attention and how to integrate the lessons learned during the struggle over the Kline's lot into a new plan of action. The focus on government complicity in downtown "development" had paid off. Yet in order to have an impact upon the structure of the local housing market, HAC believed that the emergent coalition opposed to wasteful development projects had to be turned in favor of adding significantly to the city's stock of low-income housing. HAC decided that it made sense to publicize its own analysis of the roots of homelessness as the first step toward mobilizing this support.

Walking and Talking Downtown Development

In September 1991 HAC led a group of city residents on a walking tour of the current central business district, visiting sites where low-income housing and locally owned shops and restaurants had been displaced by retail and office space serving more mobile capital with shallow ties to the community. The document produced to accompany the tour, titled "Whose Downtown Is It? Development and Displacement in Downtown Ann Arbor," includes an introduction that frames the tour as a story of the city's development, a map of the downtown with each site carefully marked, a short description of the history of each of the ten stops on the tour, and a narrative on the back page explaining how the DDA and local politicians have mutual interests in the development projects that destroyed low-income housing.

To produce this document, HAC combined historical research with political and economic analysis. HAC members conducted archival research to trace specific sites of development and displacement. Additionally, HAC took advantage of its relationship with Ann Arbor's low-income and African-American communities to draw out and develop what historian George Lipsitz calls "collective memory": the "shared experiences and perceptions about the past that legitimate action in the present." Recent downtown development had not only destroyed housing units and split up neighborhoods, it had also scattered the collective memory that Lipsitz talks about. HAC worked to assemble fragments of local history from the documents of banks and planning commissions, as well as from the memories of former downtown residents about the neighborhoods they inhabited and the social bonds they formed. By combining these various historical threads, HAC was able to create an analytical narrative about the transformation of downtown Ann Arbor. More importantly, the knowledge that went into the walking tour became part of HAC's evolving political analysis, influencing future decisions about where and how to advance the fight for low-income housing.[40]

The research and analysis that went into producing the walking tour became part of HAC's common sense about the origins of homelessness in Ann Arbor: which communities had been hardest hit by gentrification and displacement, and what would have to change to address the housing crisis. In the weeks following the public walking tour, HAC learned that the former Downtown Club, now commercial office space, was about to be foreclosed on by its lender. In November and December 1991 HAC planned and carried out an action campaign during which nineteen HAC members and supporters were arrested for trespassing in the building after opening the former Downtown Club. On three separate occasions, HAC entered the building and refused to leave until the office space was reconverted to low-income housing. Although the building was not successfully squatted and media coverage of the action was disappointing, the Downtown Club campaign led to stronger connections with Ann Arbor's African-American community, solidified ties with an emergent Union of the Homeless, and opened up a new government target—the Washtenaw County Board of Commissioners. The Board's December 1991 decision to purchase the building for use as government office space led HAC to focus its attention on the county government, which had operated up until that point in relative secrecy and anonymity.

The following spring, in April 1992, HAC and the Homeless Union established a tent city on the former site of the Salvation Army Thrift Store, calling the protest "Salvation City." Once located in the heart of the African-American business district, the Salvation Army Store was bought by the County Commissioners in 1987 and, despite requests from the Ann Arbor Shelter Association to use the building for a new day shelter, they razed it in hopes of facilitating some local development project. After the space remained vacant for over a year, the county built a "Little Park for a Little While" to fill the space until a more permanent structure could be built. For more than two months, Salvation City not only kept the problem of homelessness in the public eye and kept pressure on the county government to address the housing crisis, but it provided a history lesson by constantly reminding the community of the neighborhoods and people who had been displaced by postwar growth and development. The protest also further developed HAC's ties to the low-income and African-American communities in the neighborhoods still located around Salvation City. The lessons of Salvation City, in turn, have been incorporated into the group's collective common sense about government complicity in human suffering and about the strengths and limitations of direct action.

Analysis in the Struggle: The Lessons of Action

> *One cannot change consciousness outside of praxis. But it must be emphasized that the praxis by which consciousness is changed is not only action but action and reflection. . . . Thus there is a unity between practice and theory in which both are constructed, shaped and reshaped in constant movement from practice to theory, then back to a new practice. . . . [Conscientization] must . . . be a critical attempt to reveal reality. . . . It must . . . be related to political involvement. . . . What is more, no one conscientizes anyone else. The educator and the people together conscientize themselves, thanks to the dialectical movement which relates critical reflection on past action to the continuous struggle.*
> —Paulo Freire, "Education, Liberation and the Church"

HAC has learned that the questions generated by political struggle demand answers and that those answers lead to actions which, in turn, create new questions. This type of intellectual work is ongoing in any grass-roots community that works for social change. What makes the work of HAC exceptional is that members of HAC work as a community engaged in struggle. Not only does HAC's analysis attempt to connect the suffering of people on the streets with the political economy and priorities of the nation, but this analysis is directly and immediately applied to the group's organizing efforts. Additionally, HAC's methodology seeks to connect its members to one another, forming a collaborative research, as well as political, organization.

HAC's political work fits the model of organizing often identified with Ella Baker, a leader of the Student Nonviolent Coordinating Committee during the 1960s civil rights movement. Baker advocated "group-centered leadership," or the development of grass-roots political leaders closely connected to communities struggling for justice. According to Baker, any political struggle is not only aimed at attaining concrete goals or demands, but must also be seen as part of a larger effort to enlarge the immediate community of struggle and develop the grass-roots organizational forms and institutions that serve this end. HAC has made a conscious decision to locate its leadership within the collective that meets regularly to plan, analyze, and carry out direct action aimed toward changing the injustice of homelessness. HAC is truly a community, defined by commitment and built through the day-to-day practices of meetings, rallies, pot-luck dinners, and retreats that have enabled authentic trust to develop among a diverse group of individuals. Within this community, a common sense about political activism and democracy guides the work of the group.

To summarize, we can point to several dimensions or levels of common sense within HAC. The first level is an *analytic* common sense about homelessness which entails an analysis of development and displacement that the group tries to get out to the public through actions, speaking, and publicity—in other words the common sense that reframes homelessness as the result of structural imperatives rather than individual pathologies. Second, there is a *group process* common sense that makes consensus and the reciprocal relation between analysis and action the fundamental and unquestioned components of HAC's collective political practice. Lastly, there is a common sense about *political commitment* evident in the group's dedication to pursuing social protest as a means toward social change, an awareness that the human rights of poor people are being systematically denied them, and that the system responsible for this situation is both "unjust and mutable." This is the common sense that moves people to act to address injustice.[41] Together, analysis, group process, and commitment form a common ground upon which the group does its work: organizing and mobilizing an alliance in support of its goals, planning and carrying out actions, and evaluating successes and failures before proceeding.

We have attempted to demonstrate how HAC's common sense guides the group's activism. Within the context of Ann Arbor's transformation during the past forty-five years, HAC's work takes on significance not only because of the critique of economic development and the explanation of homelessness that the group advances, but also because of the model of intellectual work that the group has developed. In a city where the dominant form of knowledge production is the research of intellectuals affiliated with the university, and the location of the university within the local political economy makes clear the complicity of this institution in the creation of homelessness, HAC challenges the dominant position of the knowledge factory by opposing the dominant direction of economic development *and* by creating an oppositional method of knowledge production. HAC's intellectual and political synthesis—its common sense—is also in direct opposition with the ideology of the city's dominant pro-growth coalition whose common sense has created economic development policies and projects directly responsible for widespread displacement. HAC's struggle, and the struggle of all groups working for social justice, requires the intellectual and political work of articulating a common sense that challenges elitism, democratizes knowledge, and transforms society. As an example of a collective effort united by political solidarity, HAC's lessons for the status quo of the knowledge factory are clear. What HAC teaches the teachers is the importance of a politics that goes beyond the academy, and links community activism with academic work in a way that constantly challenges their artificial separation.

Notes

1. The authors would like to thank the following people for their help in the writing and revising of this paper, as well as their support of HAC's political efforts: David Scobey, Robin Kelley, Roger Rouse, Michael Peter Smith, the Southeastern Michigan Reading Group at the University of Michigan, Greg Barak, Wendy Walters, and especially, David Levenstein, who co-authored an earlier conference paper from which this article originated. We dedicate the paper to the members of HAC and their continued struggles.
2. By "gentrified leisure industry" we refer to the kind of consumer practices that

represent an economic and cultural respatialization where the leisure activities of a new urban professional class link local tastes with global economic transformations through what Sharon Zukin calls, "new organizations of consumption." Zukin, *Landscapes of Power: From Detroit to Disney World* (Berkeley: University of California Press, 1991). In Ann Arbor, the most thriving downtown retail sections feature new businesses, most of which are expensive cafes and restaurants serving gourmet coffees and fast food versions of ethnic and regional nouvelle cuisine. Borders Bookstores is about to take over a huge building vacated by Jacobsons Department Store (which has moved to the Briarwood Mall on the city's periphery), and Urban Outfitters, catering to the eclectic tastes of professionals and pre-professionals, now occupies the space of a former movie theater.

3. Thierry Noyelle and Thomas Stanback, *The Economic Transformation of American Cities*. (New Jersey: Rowman and Allanheld, 1983), p. 17. Bennett Harrison and Barry Bluestone, *The Great U-Turn: Corporate Restructuring and the Polarizing of America* (New York: Basic Books, 1988); Kim Moody, *An Injury to All: The Decline of American Unionism* (New York: Verso Press, 1988).

4. Ferol Brinkman, *The University of Michigan: An Encyclopedic Survey, Volume VI, 1940–1975* (Ann Arbor: Bentley Historical Library, 1981); University of Michigan Budget, 1949–1950 (Ann Arbor: University of Michigan Regents, June 1950); University of Michigan Budget, 1989–1990 (Ann Arbor: University of Michigan Regents, June 1990). These growth and research trends were true for most major academic research institutions after WWII. For an excellent in-depth study of two other examples see Stuart Leslie, *The Cold War and American Science: The Military-Industrial-Academic Complex at MIT and Stanford* (New York: Columbia University Press, 1993).

5. Vannevar Bush, *Science—The Endless Frontier* (New York: Arno Press, 1980); Christopher Jencks and David Riesman, *The Academic Revolution* (Garden City, New York: Doubleday & Company, 1968). It was Bush's vision that universities would become the central sites for military and commercial scientific research. Through his brainchild, the National Defense Research Committee (NDRC), the government poured millions into universities for the purpose of "basic research." But Bush himself often conflated "basic" and "applied" research by using the term "fundamental research." As Hunter Dupree has noted, this conflation was the "genius" of the NRDC because Bush knew that the key personnel for his plan, university scientists, "would rally only to the banner of fundamental [basic] research even though applications would be clearly aligned to the narrow focus of the military." Hunter Dupree, "The Great Instauration of 1940: The Organization of Scientific Research for War" in *The Twentieth Century Sciences: Studies in the Biography of Ideas*, edited by Gerald Holton (New York: W.W. Norton & Company, Inc.) pp. 448–54.

6. Brinkman, *University of Michigan Encyclopedic Survey*.

7. Chester Lang, "A Proposal to the General Electric Company" Michigan Memorial Phoenix Project Box 1, Bentley Historical Library: Ann Arbor, Michigan; Alexander Ruthven, "The President's Report, 1949" (Ann Arbor: University of Michigan, 1950); Stephen Hilgartner, Richard Bell, and Rory O'Connor, *Nukespeak: Nuclear Language, Visions, and Mindset* (San Francisco: Sierra Club Books, 1982); Richard Hewlett and Jack Holl, *Atoms for Peace and War, 1953–1961: Eisenhower and the Atomic Energy Commission* (Berkeley: University of California Press, 1989).

8. Development Council of the University of Michigan, "Suggested Plan for Launching a Corporation Program," February 1954. Development Council Box 1, Bentley

Historical Library. The Council's Board included the Chairs, Presidents, or Vice Presidents of the following corporations: the American Sugar Refining Co., the Libby Owens Ford Glass Co., Detroit Edison, Ann Arbor Trust Co., Massachusetts Mutual Life Insurance Co., Bank of Lansing, Lincoln National Life Insurance Co., General Electric, Knapt-Vogt manufacturing Co., and the Nash-Kelvinator Co.

9. J. A. Livingston, "Michigan Joins College Try For Funds From Corporations," *The Evening Bulletin*, October 26, 1954.

10. Engineering Research Institute, "Annual Report, 30," June 30, 1951 (Ann Arbor: University of Michigan).

11. Industry and Education (Detroit, General Motors, 1955) Harlan Hatcher Papers Box 10, Bentley Historical Library; "Request for Funds for University of Michigan—Dearborn Center," University of Michigan Development Office, Development Council Box 1, Bentley Historical Library.

12. Fran R. Bacon and Kenneth E. Bayer, "A Comparison of the Research Patterns of Michigan Universities with State and National Research and Industrial Trends: Research Emphasis in Michigan Universities" (Ann Arbor: Industrial Development Division, Institute of Science and Technology, 1964); J.A. Boyd, "The Industrial Development Division of the Institute of Science and Technology of the University of Michigan: Fifteen Years, 1960–1974" (Ann Arbor: Institute of Science and Technology, 1975). Of course there is an obvious self-serving nature to producing studies that support the funding of your own institution, but this is one of the many advantages of being a credentialed expert producer of knowledge in an economy that relies increasingly on knowledge production for growth.

13. David Noble, *America By Design: Science, Technology, and the Rise of Corporate Capitalism* (Oxford: Oxford University Press, 1977), p. 146

14. Alan DiGaetano and John Klemanski, "Restructuring the Suburbs: Political Economy of Economic Development in Auburn Hills, Michigan." *Journal of Urban Affairs* 13 (Number 2, 1991). Digaetano and Klemanski argue that throughout the 1970s, cities like Auburn Hills and Ann Arbor, whose economic bases were historically rooted in service industries and had research university connections, benefitted from state economic development policies. In specific, a "Blue Ribbon Commission on High Technology . . . envisioned a Southeastern Michigan version of the North Carolina Research Triangle, which would facilitate cooperative R&D ventures among the auto industry, government, and research institutions of the University of Michigan, Michigan State, Wayne State, and Oakland University."

15. Clark Kerr, *The Uses of the University* (Cambridge: Harvard University Press, 1972), p. 93.

16. Ann Arbor City Planning Commission, "Land Supply and Demand in Ann Arbor," (Ann Arbor, 1950); Jonathan Marwil, *A History of Ann Arbor* (Ann Arbor: University of Michigan Press, 1987), pp. 135–42.

17. City Planning Commission, "Land Supply and Demand"; Washtenaw County Planning Commission, "The Industry of Washtenaw" (Ann Arbor, 1949). John Mollenkopf and Michael Peter Smith and Dennis Judd make similar arguments about the federal government's conflation of growth with the public interests as part of postwar progrowth ideology that fueled urban revitalization projects. John Mollenkopf, *The Contested City* (Princeton: Princeton University Press, 1983); Michael Peter Smith and Dennis Judd, "American Cities: The Production of Ideology," in *Cities in Transformation: Class, Capital, and the State. Urban Affairs*

Annual Reviews, volume 26 (Beverly Hills: Sage Publications, 1984), pp. 173–199.

18. Marwil, "A History," pp. 138–42; William E. Brown, Jr., "State University Agrees to Payments To City in Lieu of Taxes" *Michigan Municipal Review* (December 1946), pp. 140–41.

19. Letter from William E. Brown to the Honorable Common Council of Ann Arbor, May 28, 1956, William E. Brown Papers Box 7, Bentley Historical Library.; Ann Arbor Chamber of Commerce, "The Greater Ann Arbor Research Park" Ann Arbor,1961, College of Engineering Papers Box 22, Bentley Historical Library.

20. Brown, Letter to Council, May 28, 1956.

21. Letter from John H. Swisher to William E. Brown, June 21, 1956, William Brown Papers Box 7, Bentley Historical Library.

22. Memo from Guy Larcolm to Ann Arbor Common Council, "Program For an Expanding City," January 15, 1957, William E. Brown Papers, Box 7.

23. Thomas Dickinson, "Recipe For A Research Park," *Michigan Business Review* (November, 1961), pp. 1–7.

24. Ibid, pp. 1–4.

25. Manuel Castells, *The Informational City: Information Technology, Economic Re-structuring, and the Urban-Regional Process* (Oxford: Blackwell Publishers, 1989), pp.19–31; David Harvey, *The Condition of Postmodernity* (Oxford: Blackwell Publishers, 1989), pp. 141–189. This reorganization was characterized by the trends we mentioned earlier in the article and are discussed more in depth by Corey Dolgon in "Innovators and Gravediggers: Capital Restructuring and Class Formation in a Postindustrial City," Ph.D Dissertation (Ann Arbor: University of Michigan, forthcoming).

26. Guy Larcolm, "State of the City: Address to the Chamber of Commerce, Board of Directors Organizational Meeting," January 14, 1965, Ann Arbor Chamber of Commerce Newsletter, Bentley Historical Library; Ann Arbor Chamber of Commerce Newsletter, "The challenge of '66," December 28, 1965, Bentley Historical Library.

27. Mike Davis, *City of Quartz: Excavating the Future in Los Angeles* (New York: Verso Press, 1990), pp.151–221. In Ann Arbor, this exclusivism germinates in the kind of "small town charm" that city officials still maintain characterizes the city despite its extensive postwar growth. The Chamber's "selective growth" and the need to attract "the right type" of industry relate to the necessity of trying to negotiate rapid growth with a desire for the cultural capital derived from a historic sense of small town values. For Liz Brater, Ann Arbor mayor from 1988–1990, this convergence meant a "recession-resistant" economy where new growth is "wisely balanced" with historic preservation and the downtown promotes a "cosmopolitan" atmosphere of social and cultural diversity while still offering the "best of small towns." "'Community,' 'Profitability,' and Struggle: Downtown Development in the 'City of Intellect.'" Paper presented at the Fifth National Conference on American Planning History, Society of American City and Regional Planning History, Chicago, IL November,1993.

28. Ellen Morris-Knower, "The City of Briarland," *Ann Arbor Observer* February 1991; Ann Arbor Planning Commission, "Briarwood Shopping Center: A Comprehensive Report," February 9, 1971; Hammer, Greene, and Siler, "Impact of the Proposed Briarwood Shopping Center on the Ann Arbor Retail Market," February 1971; Ann Arbor Chamber of Commerce, "Briarwood Statement," February 15, 1971. In their statement, the Chamber recognizes that perimeter growth is inevitable and supports the construction of Briarwood. However, much of the state-

ment focuses on the necessity of city government spending money to facilitate downtown revitalization projects to improve the business climate. These projects included more parking structures and a highway bypass that threatened to destroy dozens of homes in the black community.

29. Chamber of Commerce, "Challenge of '66"; Ann Arbor Human Rights Commission, "Ann Arbor Self Survey," Ann Arbor, 1956; Human Rights Commission Meeting Minutes, February 5, 1962, Cecil Creel Papers Box 2, Bentley Historical Library; Interview with Herbert O. Ellis, January 17, 1994.

30. Donald Deskins, "Negro Settlement in Ann Arbor, 1860–1960," unpublished master's thesis, University of Michigan, 1962; Human Rights Commission, "Self Survey," interview with Tony Taylor, January 6, 1994; interview with Mary Ann Hinton, July 27, 1993.

31. Deskins, "Negro Settlements," Ann Arbor City Planning Department, "Population and Housing: A Report on Population and Housing Based on the 1960 Federal Decennial Census," Ann Arbor, October, 1961; Ann Arbor City Planning Commission and the Ann Arbor Chamber of Commerce, "Guide to Action: The Ann Arbor Central Area Plan," Ann Arbor, 1963; William Ferrall, "Big Changes for North Central," *Ann Arbor Observer,* June, 1988; "Neighborhood in Transition," *Ann Arbor News,* June 14, 1992; Michael Appel, Larry Fox, and Barb Vicory, "Census Numbers Show Racial Segregation and Economic Disparity," *The Tenants' Voice: An Informational Newsletter of the Ann Arbor Tenants Union,* May–June, 1991; interview with Tony Taylor; interview with Mary Ann Hinton; interview with Sheila Tyler, July 19, 1993.

32. Ann Arbor Planning Commission and Chamber of Commerce, "A Guide to Action."

33. Ann Arbor Planning Department, "Northside Character Study," Ann Arbor, August, 1977.

34. Kim Hopper, Ezra Susser, and Sarah Conover, "Economies of Makeshift: Deindustrialization and Homelessness," *Urban Anthropology,* Volume 14 (1–3, 1985), p.184.

35. Richard Campbell and Jimmie Reeves, "Covering the Homeless: The Joyce Brown Story," *Critical Studies in Mass Communication,* 6 (1989); Neil Smith and Peter Williams, *Gentrification and the City* (Boston: Allen & Unwin, Inc., 1986); Peter Rossi, *Down and Out in America: The Origins of Homelessness* (Chicago: University of Chicago Press, 1989); Charles Hoch and Robert Slayton, *The New Homeless and Old: Community and the Skid Row Hotels* (Philadelphia: Temple University Press, 1989); Michael J. Dear, *Landscapes of Despair: From Deinstitutionalization to Homelessness.* (Princeton, NJ: Princeton University Press, 1987); Elizabeth Roistacher, "Housing Finances and Housing Policy in the United States: Legacies of the Reagan Era," in *Government and Housing* (Beverly Hills: Sage Publications, 1990).

36. Ann Arbor Citizens' Council, "Homelessness in Ann Arbor," *Citizen News* (February, 1984). Homeless Action Committee, "Whose Downtown Is It?: Development and Destruction in Downtown Ann Arbor" (Ann Arbor, 1991), p.5.

37. As Greg Barak points out, "homelessness" emerges as a product of the shift from an industrial-based economy to a postindustrial service economy and explains a "new" poverty by focusing public attention on "*individual* vulnerabilities" instead of "the *institutional* roots" of poverty. This is the hegemonic common sense about homelessness. Hoch and Slayton, *New Homeless and Old* , pp. 4–6; Greg Barak, *Gimme Shelter: A Social History of Homelessness in Contemporary America* (New York: Praeger, 1991) pp. 5–15.

Our use of the term common sense is based on our understanding of Italian Marxist Antonio Gramsci's development of the concept. By "common sense" Gramsci meant a "conception of the world uncritically absorbed by the various social and cultural environments in which the moral individuality of the average man is developed"—in other words the philosophy of the masses. Gramsci argued that the "philosophy of praxis" (his term for Marxism) must intervene on this terrain to take popular assumptions about society and "renovate" them or make them critical. For while common sense is not necessarily oppositional, neither is it static; it can be recruited to an oppositional politics or to the hegemonic social and political philosophy of a ruling bloc (Gramsci, pp. 419–25, 331).

We suggest that not only does oppositional (as well as hegemonic) politics *recruit* and *renovate* the common sense of average men and women, but that it creates and articulates its own common sense. It follows that oppositional work (our focus here) may be charted by examining the analysis that a group produces in addition to the resources that a group mobilizes. Our analysis and interpretation of HAC's political work draws upon and goes beyond the work of theorists of social movements. See, for example: Barbara Epstein, *Political Protest and Cultural Revolution: Nonviolent Direct Action in the 1970s and 1980s* (Berkeley: U.C. Press, 1991); Rick Fantasia, *Cultures of Solidarity: Consciousness, Action and Contemporary American Workers* (Berkeley: U.C. Press, 1988); Doug McAdam, *Political Process and the Development of Black Insurgency, 1930–1970* (Chicago: U. Chicago Press, 1982); Aldon Morris, *The Origins of the Civil Rights Movement: Black Communities Organizing for Change* (New York: Free Press, 1984); Aldon Morris and Carol McClurg Mueller eds., *Frontiers in Social Movement Theory* (New Haven: Yale U.P., 1992); Frances Fox Piven and Richard Cloward, *Poor People's Movements: Why They Succeed, How They Fail* (New York: Vintage, 1977); Meyer Zald and John McCarthy, *Social Movements in an Organizational Society* (New Brunswick, NJ: Transaction Press, 1987). On urban social movements, see especially Manuel Castells, *The City and the Grassroots: A Cross-Cultural Theory of Urban Social Movements* (Berkeley: U.C. Press, 1983); Mike Davis et al. eds., *Fire in the Hearth: The Radical Politics of Place in America* (London: Verso, 1990); and Michael Peter Smith and Richard Tardanico, "Urban Theory Reconsidered: Production, Reproduction and Collective Action," in *The Capitalist City*, edited by Michael Peter Smith and Joe Feagin (Oxford: Basil Blackwell Ltd., 1987).

38. Unlike large American cities whose initial period of rapid industrial growth dates to the nineteenth century, Ann Arbor does not have the significant stock of seriously deteriorated and/or abandoned housing that squatters usually target. Thus HAC's squatting campaign did not represent the beginning of a tactic that could be easily reproduced across the city. Rather, the strength of the political message that the squatted houses sent was due to the destruction and displacement the proposed lot would require. The connections between homelessness and development could hardly have been more direct than they were with the Kline's lot.

39. The decision to work on building a coalition opposing the dominant forces behind economic development was made over time at weekly meetings and at a retreat in June, 1990. Retreats are not on a calendar but are called for by members when there is a sense of need and usually happen two to three times a year. In a one-day retreat, HAC clarifies long-term and short-term goals, mapping the local political landscape and sketching out the best course forward.

40. George Lipsitz, *A Life in the Struggle: Ivory Perry and the Culture of Opposition* (Philadelphia: Temple, 1989) p. 228. Perhaps the two most instructive examples

of development and displacement included in the walking tour are the conversion of the Downtown Club (discussed above) and the demolition of the Salvation Army Thrift Store in 1989. Both of these changes took place in the neighborhood that was once the heart of Ann Arbor's African-American community, where yuppie retail development now thrives. Meanwhile, many of Ann Arbor's low-income and working-class residents have had to move to neighboring Ypsilanti, where rental prices, if not jobs, are more within reach.

41. Piven and Cloward have developed a theory of social protest movements that posits specific necessary preconditions for such movements. They write, "For a protest movement to arise out of these traumas of daily life, people have to perceive the deprivation and disorganization they experience as both wrong, and subject to redress. The social arrangements that are ordinarily perceived as just and immutable must come to seem both unjust and mutable." Piven and Cloward p. 12.

2

Tranquility City: Self-Organization, Protest, and Collective Gains within a Chicago Homeless Encampment[1]

Talmadge Wright

Homeless encampments and shelters, nesting in marginalized areas of cities and suburbs, have become more prevalent with increasing income polarization and unemployment. Encampments are often presented in the popular media as either exotic locations for the "Other," places to be feared, the urban equivalent of "wilderness," or as locations for the dispensation of charity. Rarely are homeless encampments presented as vehicles for generating community in the popular press. When community is mentioned it is often in reference to a non-normative, out of the mainstream community, one populated with disaffiliated, isolated individuals. The following account is about one set of encampments that questions the disaffiliation model of homelessness and serves to remind us of the power of community in generating new concepts of self and social change, a precursor to the formation of social movements.

From November 1991 to June 1992 "Tranquility City," a moderate-sized squatter camp of twenty-two 6 × 8 × 8 foot plywood "huts," located in a deteriorated industrial district on the Near West Side of Chicago, Illinois, housed approximately fifty homeless persons for varying lengths of time.[2] Tranquility City, a name given to this homeless encampment by one of its members, lasted almost a year until its dismantling by city authorities. Members of Chicago's homeless population mobilized community support, involving several local churches, activist groups, universities and local volunteers. As a result of negotiations with the city of Chicago all of the homeless living in the encampment received apartments in Chicago's Public Housing projects, apartments that normally take years to receive.

What began as a protest against the lack of affordable housing became a method of building community, involving homeless individuals, artists and community activists. Active protests by the homeless generated real material gains contributing to collective empowerment[3] and the formation of an organization called the People's Campaign for Jobs, Housing and Food disputing the concept of disaffiliation, often discussed in relationship to the very poor. Tranquility City, far from being an aberration, illustrated the creative capacities of those marginalized by the lack of affordable housing and decent employment. Similar to Wagner's "Politicos" (1993; Wagner and Cohen 1991) many of the hut dwellers exhibited a high degree of political consciousness and the capacity for sustained organizational work, some having participated in the early civil rights movement, another with the Black Panther Party.

What squatters gain from the self-organization of encampments and why encampments are "chosen" as opposed to shelters are questions that speak to the desire for community, autonomy, and privacy. The question of why squatting is "preferred" over shelters was a major focus for this study. The place of the unhoused and very poor is problematic in a society that prides itself on striving for the "American Dream" while denying its fulfillment to large sectors of the population. The social space that Tranquility City occupied placed it at the center of the controversy over the meaning of public space and the role of the unhoused. The resistance of those who lived in the encampments to their dispersal by the city of Chicago would not have been possible without the prior establishment of social networks throughout the community.

The extensive social networks, submerged in the everyday lives (Melucci 1989; 1988) of members of Tranquility City, those in shelters, those living on the streets of Lower Wacker Drive, and those in advocacy groups constituted a social movement of the very poor. As Melucci explains, the very form of social networking and resource mobilization that occurs among social groups is what constitutes a social movement. While Melucci wrote about the emergence of the new social movements of the 1970s and 1980s based on issues of identity, his model of social networks is useful in understanding how the residents of Tranquility City came to form a community and the implications of such a community for a social movement of the very poor. Collective action for Melucci occurs in "movement areas" which are networks "composed of a multiplicity of groups that are dispersed, fragmented and submerged in everyday life, and which act as cultural laboratories" (Melucci 1989, 60). For Melucci these are networks of groups through which individuals and information circulate. Limited part-time involvement and multiple memberships characteristic of these networks was evident in Tranquility City where different squatters worked with a local church, schools, and different advocacy groups. Several different grassroots organizations were directly involved with Tranquility City including the Mad Housers of Atlanta, the Chicago Coalition for the Homeless, local churches, and art galleries.

For a brief period Tranquility City became a *mini-movement area* in which a different way of living poor was experimented with; a possibility was created for the formation of a homeless community free of institutional shelter restraints. Within this mini-movement, area residents of Tranquility City were able to construct a collective identity centered around issues of social justice for other homeless individuals and collective action in helping each other acquire housing and needed services. Therefore collective gains were not simply individual gains, but, social gains leading to new beliefs in the legitimacy of organizing. The assumption that the very poor lack knowledge and social affiliation with mainstream institutions and social groups was simply not true for Tranquility City residents. Lack of meaningful well-paid employment and housing is a better explanatory factor for their marginalization.

Methods

Participant-observation at the site, from the time of the encampment's conceptualization in October 1991 to the time of its closing in June of 1992, and in-depth semi-structured interviews with participants were utilized to gather data. In addition, newspaper accounts were gathered and news reporting monitored. During this time period weekly visits were made to the site by both myself and student researchers using techniques borrowed from Rosenthal's method of "hangin' out" (1991). Data gathered from observations were supported by interviews with thirteen of the thirty-six who we were initially informed had been involved in the encampments, and seven with those who were indirectly involved.[4] Interviews were conducted at a local homeless advocacy office and in the Chicago public housing projects, after the squatters had received housing. We were informed by former squatters that as of February 1994 only five known members had returned to the streets out of those who had received housing.

For the remainder of this paper I would like to outline a brief history of Tranquility City, its inception, development, and demise, followed by an examination of its impact upon those squatters who received housing, social motivations, gains achieved, and attitudes about the shelter system that led many of them to seek this form of housing in the first place.

The Near West Side and Tranquility City

The Near West Side has traditionally been the repository of social services and the historic home of "skid row." Caught between the forces of redevelopment, oriented towards large projects such as Presidential Towers and the designed West Side Stadium, a declining industrial base, and an area of mixed economic activity, the Near West Side provided a location, a home to many of those living on the streets. During the preceding ten years the Near West Side, as well as other parts of the city of Chicago has experienced a rapid decline in cheap, inexpensive housing most often associated with "flop houses" and Single-Room Occupancy hotels (SROs). The process of gentrification and redevelopment exaggerated the move to demolish old SROs in the wake of the decline of earlier transient worker populations (Hoch 1989; Marcuse 1989; Thomas and Wright 1990; Kasinitz 1986). In addition, the decline of inexpensive movie houses made it difficult for local homeless individuals to sleep undisturbed during the day. The emergence of Tranquility City was a logical extension to the homeless community that had existed in embryonic form around the Fulton Street market area, at Lake and Green Street, for many years.

While Chicago's overall median household income increased from $25,644 in 1979 to $26,301 in 1989, the Near West Side witnessed a rapid drop in median income, from $10,188 in 1979 to $9,336 in 1989, and an 80 percent decline in population. Those who did move into the area were predominantly middle-class professionals. According to the 1990 Census, those households working in skilled middle-class occupations requiring advanced educations such as managers, sales, and finance experienced the largest growth: 25 percent, 32 percent, and 55 percent respectively from 1980 to 1990. Households associated with working-class occupations, machine operators, assemblers, inspectors (–31 percent), durable goods manufacturing (–44 percent), and health services (–68 percent) decreased dramatically. In addition, those households which labored as low skilled workers, such as handlers, equipment cleaners, helpers, and handlers decreased 57 percent. Within this depressed economic area one can find squatters and homeless individuals mixing with the new influx of artists and a scattering of young urban professionals.

In light of the above structural transformations it is informative to note that of the people interviewed only two were still working and those positions were both part-time and low-paying day labor or service jobs. Prior employment for squatter residents consisted of construction, sand blasting, machinist, cab driving, cook, fork lift driver, telecommunication sales (part time) and day labor. Most of the squatters received small benefits, either SSI, food stamps or General Assistance. Prior work periods ranged from a low of one month to thirteen years. Work tended to be episodic and unstable. When asked about their father's occupations all squatters with the exception of one person from Africa listed working-class occupations (railroad worker, cargo ship worker, truckdriver, construction, bartender, and farmer). Mother's occupation was listed as housewife except for three who stated that their mothers worked in a factory, as a waitress, or as a teacher in Africa. With the exception of several African-American females, one white, and two Latinos, all squatters were middle-aged African-American males with a median age of forty-three.

History of Tranquility City

The history of Tranquility City represents the confluence of several different social vectors in a city believed to have approximately 20–60,000 homeless. Homeless advocacy groups, local shelters, the Chicago arts community, property owners, local churches and universities, and of course the homeless themselves were the main actors in the emergence of the encampment. Starting in September 1991, a local art gallery, Randolph Street Gallery, began a series of forums devoted to "Counter-Proposals: Adaptive Approaches to a Built Environment." The Mad Housers of Atlanta, Georgia were invited to conduct workshops and seminars on low-cost housing for the poor and to develop homeless "huts" that could be used in Chicago. Over 200 huts were built in Atlanta in prior years. After their arrival the Mad Housers contacted both the local Coalition for the Homeless and a new group, Homeless on the Move for Equality (HOME), established by those homeless who had been evicted from the O'Hare airport. Simultaneously, a local graphic artist who walked the railroads near his house spotted squatters living nearby in an abandoned warehouse and began to befriend them, eventually inviting them to meetings with the Mad Housers at the art gallery.

Throughout the month of October 1991 debates about where to locate the first huts and their purpose took place. The Mad Housers attempted to dovetail their efforts with that of the Coalition for the Homeless. The Coalition was conducting a campaign against the lack of affordable housing at Presidential Towers, a high rise federally subsidized luxury housing project that excluded the poor. Initial plans suggested locating the huts at the Towers. Other ideas included siting the huts in wealthier North Side neighborhoods to make a point about the lack of affordable housing. All of these were rejected as causing problems for the homeless population itself. Finally, it was decided to locate the huts where some of the street people were already staying, near the Fulton Street markets, on Chicago Milwaukee Corporation property adjacent to the suburban Metra railway lines. Local homeless men attended meetings of the Mad Housers at the gallery in preparation for receiving their huts. The actual design workshop in which the first huts were built was conducted October 31 followed by siting the huts on the Near West Side. The initial huts, given to two middle-aged homeless men, who slept under the docks next to a warehouse they named "Pallet City," prompted the construction of more huts, as the word filtered out through the shelter system and on the streets. By June of 1992 there were a total of eighteen huts established within a three-block perimeter.

With the publication of a February article in the *Chicago Sun-Times* (Smith 1992) concerning the Mad Housers and the encampment, Tranquility City assumed a high public profile. At this time the city of

Chicago gave tacit permission for their presence. According to spokeswoman, Avis La Velle: "We haven't had any complaints from property owners—and without complaints, the mayor sees no reason to tear them down" (Smith 1992, 4). In addition, Metra rail gave their okay to the settlement.[5]

During this period members of HOME patrolled Lower Wacker Drive talking to local street people about the huts and the alternative to the shelters as well as recruiting homeless individuals to vote. Other homeless individuals not affiliated with HOME would meet with the Mad Housers and go to the shelters to spread the word about the huts. In the discussions between the Mad Housers, community activists, and members of the local homeless population it was emphasized that the huts were not a solution, but rather a way of making a symbolic statement about homelessness. The Mad Housers understood their role as builders, to provide temporary housing, to conduct guerrilla architecture. The homeless residents were of a more diverse mind, perceiving the building of the huts as both a symbolic gesture, a protest, and a way to stabilize their own lives, a place of security and privacy. Many of them had been homeless for over six months, some as many as ten years, others as little as four months, exhibiting a high degree of street knowledge. This contradiction in intent I believe came to fruition in the final struggles over Tranquility City when it was condemned by the city of Chicago.

With the onset of spring weather, the city of Chicago had a change of heart. According to the mayor's spokesperson, "The Mayor has decided that it is not in the best interest of the city to allow these structures" (Smith 1992a). Citing problems of lack of running water, sanitary facilities, and electricity the city was eager to dispose of the huts, even though no complaints had been filed. As Commissioner Dan Weil commented, "It is clear they're not safe. They don't have permits. They don't have plumbing. They don't meet the code. They're coming down . . . If those huts were allowed to exist, then why should anyone have to obtain a permit for anything" (Smith 1992b). These reasons were received with much indignation from the local homeless community who believed that it was their visibility combined with support from commuting suburbanites and community activists and a proposed redevelopment plan for the area that precipitated Mayor Daley's decision. Speculation abounded in the papers about a proposal to build a new "urban Ravinia" and casino near the huts location.

According to Robert Wiggs, executive director of the West Central Association, a group representing property owners in the area, "we might call it a type of necessary displacement" (Smith 1992c). Any connection between developer's interests and the dismantling of the huts were denied by the city. It was clear that other areas of the Near West Side occupied by shelters were also feeling the squeeze of gentrification. While the city of Chicago said that it had no plans to close any of the shelters in the area, local business people and incoming neighbors were disturbed by the presence of large numbers of homeless in the area (Stein 1992).

It should be said that the huts, well ventilated, with thick insulation from the cold, a sleeping loft with window and storage space, and an internal stove that doubled as a range and heater kept the squatters warm in subfreezing weather and provided security and privacy by having locks on all of the doors. Showers were taken at a local shelter and running water was taken from a fire hydrant that a city worker had turned on for the squatters. The huts were clearly visible during the winter months from the luxury apartment windows of nearby Presidential Towers.[6]

With notice that their huts were being taken down the squatters organized a campaign bringing public attention to the plight of the homeless throughout the city of Chicago. The human services commissioner, Daniel Alvarez began negotiations with the squatters and promised that "there would be no bulldozers" (Thorton 1992). Instead the huts were lifted on the back of flatbed trucks and taken away.

While the Christian Industrial League, one of many shelters offering overnight and transitional housing, referred to the problem as one of lack of information—the "homeless don't know how to access the system"—and encouraged them to come into the shelter system rather than be on the streets, the squatters themselves had other ideas. Ranging from rehabilitating abandoned buildings to moving into apartments, all of the homeless in our small sample refused any residency in a homeless shelter for reasons which we shall talk about below. The understanding of the squatter perspective by shelter providers takes the form of one in which the squatter is labeled as recalcitrant, of not wanting to follow the rules against no alcohol, of being in at certain hours, and leaving early in the morning. Unfortunately this disciplinary agenda of social control conflicts with the squatter's desire for privacy, autonomy, and freedom, the ability to come and go when he or she pleases, and the security of being able to lock up one's possessions.[7]

As the City negotiated with the squatters on alternatives to hut housing two more huts went up bringing the original 16 to 18 in the immediate area by the end of May. During negotiations with the City, the Mad Housers were often given a high profile role, a role which occasionally clashed with the squatters themselves. Both groups were united against the City's efforts to displace the squatters, with the Mad Housers joined by The Architects Designers Planners for Social Responsibility and the Coalition for the Homeless. As negotiations progressed with the Mad Housers the squatters were offered public housing as replacement housing. The attempt by the city to deal with the Mad Housers as opposed to the squatters brought sharp reactions from the homeless. According to one of the squatters, "They keep wanting to bring the Mad Housers into the meetings, but we're capable of telling them our needs" (*Chicago Tribune* June 2, 1992, Sec. 2, 3).[8] This precipitated a refusal on the part of some of the squatters to tour Chicago Housing Authority housing as an alternative. While promising not to take away any of the huts during negotiations, the city confiscated seven huts on June 10 and relocated their residents in various public housing projects. The squatters wanted the huts to remain to house other homeless street people after they moved into new dwellings. However, for the city, according to Human Services Commissioner Daniel Alvarez, "I don't know what they are complaining about. We said we weren't going to bulldoze those huts. And we're not. But after relocating these people, what's the use of having those wood boxes there? We are simply trying to clear the area of debris" (Smith 1992d).[9] Homeless squatters were dispersed and relocated to Lathrop Homes, Rockwell Gardens, Washington Park Homes, and the Wicker Park Apartments, according to their preference.

As the Tranquility City squatters dispersed into Chicago's public housing some became more organized by establishing the People's Campaign for Jobs, Housing, and Food. They have continued to search out other homeless persons to encourage them to take an apartment in public housing. Since telephones are scarce, lines of communication were kept open through leaving messages and talking to neighbors. In addition, they scheduled a Labor Day reunion of Tranquility City supporters and former members a year later at the same site. Over two dozen people celebrated "Remember: Tranquility City."

Shelters, the Street, and Respect

In 1993, Chicago's shelter system served 18,781 unduplicated clients while emergency services served 3,341 (City of Chicago 1994, 33), 60 percent of whom are African-Americans. While 40 percent of homeless persons are in families, our population consisted of single adults. Single adults constituted 80 percent of those in Department of Human Services shelters in 1993, both overnight and transitional. Homeless youth were not represented in our encampment, or indeed in cursory observations of Lower Wacker Drive where some of the hut dwellers had stayed before securing a hut.

Staying in shelters was highly problematic for Tranquility City residents. Many of the squatters had spent time in the shelter system. Their attitudes were mixed. As members of a community considered to have what Goffman referred to as "spoiled identities" (1963), homeless individuals have to cope with various types of "degradation ceremonies" (Garfinkel 1956) in order to use shelter services.[10] This may mean extensive screening for drug or alcohol use, whether or not one engages in its consumption, limiting the hours spent at the shelter, obeying curfew limits, sleeping in cramped quarters with others who may rob you, dealing with abuse from security guards, and other behaviors which impinge upon one's sense of dignity, respect and freedom. Homeless individuals cope by resorting to various tactics "alternating between resistance and manipulation, accommodation and avoidance" (Wagner 1993, 98). Quite often non-professional service providers, as pointed out by Robertson (1991), are unable to furnish the necessary level of care to the homeless community. This may account for why many of the squatters perceived some shelters as better than others.[11]

Shelters were perceived as only places of last resort, places that were perceived as dangerous for one's body as well as one's self respect.[12] The apparent arbitrary nature of shelter rules is perceived by the squatters as abusive. According to one squatter:

The shelters . . . that's strange thing because each one has its own rules. If you got a sandwich, you can't come in with a sandwich, you can't go out with a sandwich . . .

You never know what the rules are?

Right. They might bar you out. It might be five below zero out there and you got a sandwich in your pocket and the security guard sees you with a sandwich and you're barred out. You feel pretty bad then. All of a sudden you gotta hit the streets for having a sandwich in your pocket. I've seen that happen.[13]

As institutions of social control shelters often impose a disciplinary agenda coded in extensive rules combined with attempts to maximize use of the limited resources at hand. Often short of help and money, underfunded shelters find themselves caught between a "moral agenda" to reform the individual and the need to maintain order within the shelter. The keeping of order may be entrusted to nonprofessionals, often previously homeless individuals, who may abuse their new found authority. The squatters talked much about how homeless individuals are "talked down to" by security guards. Tim commented:

I went to the shelter over here, Sousa House, Me and Wayne. They had this off duty guy there who worked for Cook County jail and anytime he would just come in there and this guy would talk just as nasty. He would say, "If you don't stand in line, you can get the hell out of here!" He would threaten people. He had a mixed crowd. You have some people that love to have that power, that authority telling you what to do. But if a man ever tells me what to do then I'm out of here. And I have been to a lot of shelters. Even the staff try to tell me that I have to take an alcohol blood test. I don't have to take the test, I don't drink. Then I have to come to you and ask you for a pair of jeans because I have to go to work and you say "I'm busy right now, come back around four or five hours later." Why are you abusing your power when you can help me? The shelters only do one thing. They're concerned about one thing—their payroll and their staff. . . . These are people that love authority. To have power over other people. To dominate you and to abuse you. They talk to you like they want to and you can't say nothing in return and if you do you're out of here.[14]

Aside from the perceived *arbitrary use of power* and the maneuvering through complex sets of behavioral rules many of the shelters were thought to be controlled by gangs who made life difficult for the homeless. This was especially true around the time when disability checks were delivered.[15] Some of the shelters acknowledged this as a problem but maintained that the problem had been corrected.[16] For the squatters this was not convincing. Jack said, "homeless shelters are unsafe. They're run by gang bangers. It's like being in prison. You can't do what you want to do. You have to go to bed at 10:30 and wake up at 5:30 and they throw you outside right away. You're better living on the streets." Aside from the extensive regulations and the fear of physical violence and robbery shelters were perceived as places where you *could not rest*, where life was constant movement and disruption. The inability to stay up late prohibits night employment and the early morning rush to the showers means getting up at day-break in freezing cold weather. According to a squatter:

> They depress you more than anything. If you're going to bed at night you gotta be in by nine and then you have to be out at five thirty in the morning and it's ten below zero. It's cold and you got nowhere to go. And it's on first come first serve basis. If they fill up then you don't get in at all. As soon as you take your shower and go to sleep it seems like it's time for you to get out again.[17]

There is also a recognition by the squatters that shelters are inadequately funded and lack the programs necessary to assist in long-term stability. This was reflected in comments about inadequate food and unsanitary conditions. Some squatters mentioned getting lice in those shelters that did not change blankets frequently. However, squatters praised those shelters that have instituted extensive programs. Those shelters that just "warehouse" the homeless are avoided. What squatters perceive as minor infractions of the rules (for example, against drinking) shelter staff perceive as evidence of "moral disorder," behavior subject to punishment.[18] This has led many of the squatters to compare shelters with prisons in which one is robbed of any self-respect and only authority rules.[19] Tom related a story that conveys the perception of shelters as prison:

> They don't treat you right. It's like being in jail. They don't want to hear nothing you got to say and they don't really care about you. It's a job to them. For most of them it's just a job. Sometimes I've seen them treat people really bad. The police found a guy in an alley one day and they brought him to a shelter. He had blood all over himself and he was in really bad shape. I know for a fact that day they had clothes and stuff and a place where you could shower. But they turned him away because he didn't have a card or something. He didn't even come to stay! He just wanted to shower and get some clean clothes. The police brought him there to keep him from going to jail. He was barefoot and everything. They turned him away. On one occasion this guy had been drinking a lot and somebody had robbed him. He didn't have any shoes on and he just had a pair of pants and no shirt. It was kind of cold out, too. Everybody looked at him and laughed at him and they turned him away, too. I gave him a t-shirt out of my bag. If I'd had some shoes I would have gave him the shoes. They don't really care about the people in the shelters. They help where the point where they give you a place to sleep and something to eat but they don't really care. It's just a job to them.

While shelters were places to be avoided at all cost the squatters never had sufficient money to afford their own apartment or room, since many of the SROs that could have provided housing were either too expensive or had been destroyed. The only place for the very destitute in order to avoid the shelter system was the streets and/or public housing. Issues of respect, being treated with dignity and having the freedom to make one's own decisions separate those who used shelters extensively from those who live on the streets, according to the squatters.[20]

Internalization of Status Differences

What shelter providers treat as a minor inconvenience, following certain rules, the squatters perceive as a major attack on their self-respect. Tim commented about those living in shelters:

> the people in the mission always have their hand out. They want you to abide by their rules and regulations. This is for homeless people. Homeless people got rules and regulations. Why should I do that when I can have all the freedom in the street to do what I want to do? I can feed myself. I can take care of myself. I been doing this all my life and they can do it, too. These are people who want dependability. They like handouts and stuff like that.

For the squatters, the structure of authority within the shelters and their disadvantage at being on the streets relative to being in the shelter makes issues of respect a prime site for daily resentment. Aside from obeying what are percived as arbitrary enforcement of shelter rules the squatters also felt that young people telling older individuals what to do with their lives and time was a sign of disrespect. According to one of the squatters:

> For instance, I go out to the Chicago Taste here and at the Windy City job service there are guys that have been working late for them for years. And when the taste started we had all these little Irish guys, white guys, from over in Bridgeport. Here's a nineteen, eighteen year old, seventeen year old school kid trying to tell a fifty year old guy what to do and this guy (himself) already know what to do. You can't tell me nothing like that. I know what I'm doing. Don't set no rules for nobody.[21]
>
> So do you think the rules that the shelters set are in part demeaning?
>
> Yes, it takes away all respect. You can see something wrong and if you say something about it and they don't want you there. Yet they still collect the money for bringing you in there.

The issue of respect extends to what one is expected to do within the shelters. One of the squatters mentioned how resentful he felt at always having to take a breath test for alcohol when he didn't drink. He was resentful at having to use the same apparatus that other shelter people had to use. It would mean placing himself in the same position as those who use the shelters, that is to embrace the loss of one's self-respect. Every attempt to satisfy a human need, whether it is securing clothes, or a bed for the night is met, from the squatter perspective, with degrading procedures and extended waits that communicate the homeless individuals worthlessness.[22] Homelessness is not simply being without a home, but also involves a way of acting that communicates to others one's worthlessness. According to one encampment resident:

> Some people act like they're homeless. You see, when you lose your respect you might as well just lay down and die. All I got left now is my respect. Nobody gonna' take that from me. Nobody else. Some people have lost all of their dignity and respect. I sympathize with these people and I'm just glad I'm not like that. I'm different from most of the homeless people. You see some people, like the people who lived on the street are more private and secure people and they know how to act and they're different from the ones that go to the shelters. Because they're always looking for handouts and they can just scream and holler and this and that.

In so far as shelter providers are dispensing charity instead of "social justice" they are perceived by squatters as "poverty pimps," as part of a shelter industry. Rather than acting as a base to organize around issues of social justice, such as more housing, employment, and better health care, shelters serve a custodial function, the modern-day poorhouse for those unable to compete in the marketplace. Beholden to their benefactors, usually through city grants and charitable contributions, shelters are placed in a bind that limits their ability to become more political. The fear of reduced contributions is ever present. Shelters are a poor substitute for adequate housing, in particular a poor substitute for Single Room Occupancy (SRO) type housing.

Tranquility City: A Heterotopia of Resistance

Rest homes, prisons and psychiatric hospitals constitute what Foucault termed heterotopias of deviation, spaces where deviation from constructed norms is expected (Foucault 1986). Crisis heterotopias, in contrast are "privileged or sacred or forbidden places, reserved for individuals who are, in relation to society and to the human environment in which they live in a state of crisis" (Foucault 1986, 24).

Shelters would fit between these two extreme types of social spaces, both crisis and deviation, although, according to Timmer (1988) shelter organization, ideology and function closely resembles correctional facilities. In contrast the self-organization exhibited by the hut dwellers indicates a social space more closely associated with what I would term heterotopias of resistance, following Ruddick (1990). The hut dwelling community is a social space within which one can experience a different relationship to external authority and power. The image of the shelter as public, unsafe, unsanitary, and degrading contrasts sharply with the squatter's perceptions of privacy, autonomy and respect within Tranquility City.[23]

Tim, one of the first ones sleeping next to "Pallet City," the future site for the huts, stated that he chose this spot to sleep over others because, "It was a nice place, It was around trees and it was a beautiful area. It was scenic. . . . It was safe . . . Privacy, security, and safety." Others also commented on the quiet nature of the location, with the exception of the constant stream of Metra trains to the suburbs. While Tim received his hut through attending the Mad Houser meetings and meeting a local graphic artist, other hut dwellers drifted into the encampment through street contacts from Lower Wacker Drive and through the shelter grapevine. Some began to double up as shelters began to close with the onset of summer weather. Those who received huts were obligated to attend the Mad Houser meetings in order to receive them and to assist in their construction at the site. At the beginning HOME worked with several of the men at the site, drawing several more who were sleeping in Grant Park and under Lower Wacker Drive into meetings with the Mad Housers in order to receive a hut.

The huts location was bisected by the Metra railway lines and presented contrasting close-up views of both the Loop skyline, shiny glass office buildings, with abandoned brick factory buildings nearby, tall bushes, trees, and some wildlife, including many rabbits.[24] As one hut dweller remarked:

> The most beautiful place I'd ever been in life. It was peaceful. We had every type of animal there. We had all types of animals including rats, woodpeckers, cats, dogs - we had all of them. I miss that place. I think about that place often.[25]

Another hut dweller remarked that he was initially resistant to joining the camp after staying in the shelters. But what convinced him was the desire for independence and the presence of friends:

It was better than the Mission and what have you. I was very hesitant about it at first because I didn't think. . . . Well who's going to break wood in the dead of winter to stay warm and all that. Once I went there with him one night. He was out breaking wood and getting the hut warm. I was still very hesitant, because it was very cold at that time and my feet were freezing. I don't know what made me go back, but I went back. When I went back I eventually got use to cooking on a wood burning stove and to me it felt a little bit more independence than standing in a long line to get into shelters, waiting for people to feed you, sleeping with 200 or so men.

The sense of peace, a location in which one could think and repair their lives contrasts with not only the world of the shelters, but also the world of the public housing project into which the hut dwellers were placed. Several of the former hut dwellers remarked about having to constantly watch their backs around the projects due to drug dealing and gang members. One remarked about the public housing project he was in:

I hate this place. I hate to say that. I hate this place. I use to get off of work and just go to the store where we were by the railroad tracks. It didn't bother me to go to the store. I didn't have to look behind my back to see if there was anybody behind me that was going to rob me or hit me in the back of my head or something like that. It's like now when I'm over here, although you try not to give that feeling . . . you nervous, worried on what's around you. But it's a very uncomfortable feeling.[26]

Privacy, the ability to lock one's door and have the freedom to not interact with other hut dwellers if desired was highly prized by the squatters. *Autonomy* and the *freedom* to come and go when one pleases was another quality which was highly valued. Many of the squatters worked at odd jobs requiring working odd hours in off hour shifts. However, the one factor that seemed consistent for all the squatters was the *desire for safety*. The shelters were believed to be unsafe, a place where one could not protect themselves from predatory elements. In such a dense social situation the squatters felt compelled to respond to slights and insults, but knew that a response might get them thrown out in the streets. According to a squatter, "Out here you don't have to do nothing to nobody. They'll (people in shelters) get you for no reason at all. If you don't fit in they'll get you. The gangs get you."[27] The inability to defend oneself in the face of predatory behavior pushed many of the squatters out of the shelters and into the camps. According to Tim, "You never know when the next guy next to you would go off. If you protected yourself from this person you were barred from the mission and this guy would stay. So it was like your hands was tied. So that was my main reason for getting out of the mission. I was tired of that plus I was tired of not being able to work when I had to."

On the other hand, one squatter commented that one chooses to be in a shelter, "If you don't like it you ain't gotta be there. It ain't like if you was in jail. It ain't like they makin' you be there." He remarked that one has to be a man and stand up for himself. The situation of dire poverty accentuates this split between the desire to "be like a man," which is translated as seeking autonomy and self-respect through independence, and the necessity to be a shelter dependent, a part of the "people warehouse."

Tranquility City as Community

The rapid development of community, what one squatter called a subcity, depended upon the integration of the hut dwellers with the surrounding city community. As individuals they recognized their lack of power. However, the construction of eighteen huts in close proximity, combined with the extensive social networks established on the streets and through the shelters provided a locus for the establishment of collective empowerment. More than one squatter talked about their fellow squatters as "family." Squatters constantly kept in contact with each other. As John mentioned, "We would always keep in contact with each other, making sure that each other had what we needed, whether it be food, clothing, or what have you." Items brought into camp would be shared and swapping was commonplace:

> If I have a piece of pie, and I know that your with me and I know that your hungry. Your goin' to get half of that piece of pie. If I have a dollar and your with me and I know that you have really been trying and I know your trying to do something to obtain your going to get half of that 50 cents. It's called sharing . . .

This mutual support was perceived by the squatters not as a luxury but as necessary for their own survival. As one squatter said, "As a group we stuck together because we had nobody else." Conversation became a key point for communicating with each other, an arena in which one could be safe, unlike the shelters where one could say the "wrong" thing and set off a chain of events outside of one's control. Decisions were made collectively, although some newcomers would often exclude themselves, living on the farther edges of the camp. They were still checked upon by the others but were left alone. If a problem arose it would be worked out collectively. According to Howard:

> If I was in my hut and I was having problems, like for example someone was talking about pouring gasoline on my hut. I started whistling for Jim and Jim will come and assist me along with the other sixteen or seventeen other brothers and we would deal with that problem right then and there.

The close proximity of the markets near Lake Street provided occasional employment in addition to discarded food. When fire department personnel turned on a local fire hydrant the squatters could access fresh water to rinse and cook their food over their wood burning stoves. The ability to cook one's own food was important both to the squatters self-image of independence and because it put distance between themselves and what they perceived as the institutional food of the shelters. As one squatter said:

> We ate better than Pacific Garden Missions would feed you or Sousa House or Cooper's Place or Olive Branch because we had the Fulton Market. We'd sit up there and roast the meat. We were eating better outside than in the shelter. I sat down one damn night and I cried.

With media coverage and word getting out about the encampment on the street many people from the larger Chicago community became involved. This involvement was crucial to the establishment of Tranquility City as a community versus just a collection of individual huts. The relationship of the hut dwellers to others was not confined to themselves but extended to a much broader network.[28] This provided for a sense of collective empowerment, a knowledge that collectively they were being listened to as opposed to the individual isolation of the shelters. According to Wayne:

> We have all kind of people, we have different various homeless organizations, we have unions, you have people from the churches all different churches-Chicago Coalition for the Homeless, Illinois Coalition to end Homelessness, HOME, ASCME, you have various different church groups Catholic, Lutheran, Baptist churches, various students from colleges that participate-Northwestern, Loyola, Columbia, Roosevelt, all kinds of college students participating.

Unlike those homeless who have been tagged as disaffiliated, the squatters were quite conscious of mainstream norms and resources. For the squatters the recognition that others were concerned and actively took steps to assist fostered a larger sense of community that went beyond the small encampment. This sense of a larger community combined with the struggles over retaining the huts produced a greater understanding and political consciousness, an understanding which existed in weak form prior to the camp. I shall discuss this under gains achieved. For many of the squatters these outside supporters, bringing food, clothing, blankets, pots, pans, and conversation, were not simply attempting to do good, but in the squatters eyes, "they became a part of us." This generation of a larger sense of community continues with the work being done to house homeless people through the People's Campaign for Jobs, Housing and Food, an organization which emerged out of the encampment. As Tim put it:

> After we built the huts people started comin' in. We really got wrapped up into helping people then. We got totally wrapped up. We got so wrapped up that we came into the political arena with the mayor and governor and whoever else was involved. We started getting people into houses. You see us, we got houses today. And we got lots of people that we're still trying to get houses for.

The effect of this attention and of the cooperative relationships which characterized the camp, inspired many squatters to ask questions such as "what did we want?" and to encourage each other to try and find work. According to John, "I think more or less what we did was motivate each other to help themselves."[29] The movement of Tranquility City from a form of personal survival to one of political protest for "all homeless people" was swift.[30] After the Mayor reneged on his promise to allow the huts to stay, the squatters were faced with the real prospect of ending up back in the shelter system. This possibility catalyzed most of them to act in unison against the city's wishes. A strategy was formulated in how to deal with the city and the proposal acted upon by the squatters. According to Wayne, one of the squatter organizers:

> We decided to have a meeting and we decided, after the city was planning to— after the mayor wanted to renege on his promise, and so what we did, we all agreed in accord, that we would take our stance and not move until we get housing for not only the eighteen huts but as many homeless individual as we can and to make homeless issues an ongoing thing to get houses.

The effects of this type of opposition on the public were not lost to the homeless squatters. They were well aware of the media publicity surrounding the decision to take down the huts and saw that as an opportunity for non-homeless people to realize, "that you don't have a disease, that you are an intelligent person and that it's just an economical situation that you're in."

It is important to remember that Tranquility City was not completely unified nor homogenous. Factions that developed would often reintegrate into the group. New squatters, often from nearby shelters, would be allowed into the camp resulting in a "doubling up." The further distance from the original huts one was, the more likely one felt on the "margins" of decision making and resource distribution. In addition, new recruits from the streets would often bring their habits with them creating problems for other camp members. Squatters from the Eastern encampments, near the Kedzie Bridge, were attempting to panhandle near the other camps where traffic was more frequent. This created friction in the camps.[31] While these differences could often be worked out it did generate the conditions for developing factions. One squatter said in reference to perceived differences between his side of the camp and the initial huts:

> I think they were different. They were on their own. They had their own ways. I didn't associate with them because I wasn't around that much.
>
> How were they different?
>
> They had like their own city.
>
> So you felt like you were on the margins of that then?
>
> Yeah.

However, it is important to note that these squatters were more closely self-identified with the Mad Housers than Tim, Wayne or John. This point was brought out time and again during the interviews. This difference stemmed from the conflicts between the Mad Housers, the squatter leaders and the city during negotiations over what to do with the huts.

The Mad Housers perceived their role in the camp as a limited one. Their purpose was to build huts and to raise popular consciousness. This limited role was resented by many of the squatters who felt that not only did the Mad Housers abandoned them when the huts were built, rarely returning for visits, but they took the initial lead in negotiating with the city of Chicago as to the status of the huts.[32] The squatters claiming ownership over the huts wanted to represent themselves. Some squatters wanted the Mad Housers to represent them to the city, the majority did not.[33] According to squatter members the city eventually shifted its negotiations to the squatters themselves when the squatters began to display a united front. As one of the squatters put it:

> We were talking to various people, asking them what they want. We didn't say you are going to do this or else. We asked a question and the reply was they wanted to take a stance on this to get affordable housing. There were three people that they wanted the Mad Housers to represent them and we were dismayed at the time with their decision because we wanted to take a stance as a whole. United. But what we decide to do was, since we had the majority of the people living in the hut; we decided to take a stance. We will work with that. We couldn't break nobodies arms an make them do what we wanted to. But eventually as the ball got rolling the Department of Human Services and the city and various other organizations such as Chicago Housing Authority started working with the hut people. These three individuals who wanted to go astray finally jumped on the band wagon and decided that we were making the right move. In that we managed to . . . instead of housing 18 people we managed to house 51.

While the initial foray of the Mad Housers into the homeless community was met with enthusiasm the lack of inclusion of hut dwellers on the Mad Houser board met with resentment. The underlying understanding of many of the squatters was that the Mad Housers wanted to help, but not get too close to the actual homeless. John mentioned that while he admired the Mad Houser's intentions he felt they started, "looking at plywood instead of human beings."[25] While it appears that the Mad Housers sought to generate public awareness over the issue of homelessness and to provide what they term "guerrilla housing," this did not go far enough in the eyes of the squatters who developed a larger sense of community out of their political action. For the squatters it was not enough to just build huts and expose the problem of homelessness. It was also necessary to generate a base for resistance, a base from which one can capture political attention. According to Tom:

> They really pay attention to you, then. Just walking around on the street ain't gonna do it. You've got to build a foundation out there like we did. Then they start noticing you. Other than that, just walking down the street begging. . . . You've got to really come together and act like you really want something.

Collective and Individual Gains

Both material gains in the form of apartments and nonmaterial gains in the form of increased levels of respect, political awareness, and increased communication skills were all noted by the squatters as a result of their involvement with Tranquility City. Clearly the squatters, unlike much of the research on the homeless, expressed a sense of active agency and affiliation with established institutions. The conception of the homeless as a demobilized, helpless, and out of touch population found in the work of Roper (1988) and Rossi (1989) was not born out in our sample. Tent city inhabitants in Portland, Maine (Wagner and Cohen 1991; Wagner 1993), Santa Barbara, California's street population (Rosenthal 1989; 1994), Los Angeles's homeless youth squats (Ruddick 1990), and street people in Austin, Texas (Snow and Anderson 1993), all exhibit many of the same responses and activism as our own sample. Indeed, not only were the squatters in Tranquility City affiliated with mainstream institutions, but also demonstrated the self-organizational capacity to resist and negotiate for themselves over needed resources.

While all of the squatters mentioned their gain as material they also mentioned a gain in forms of collective empowerment related to a belief in organizing as a way to achieve change. As Frank put it, "Some guys get together and you say, 'Look, if we can get together the politicians will listen.' But one person can't do too much. I was always a single type person and now if somebody comes to me and says, 'Hey, we can get together . . . ' I'll listen now."[35] In addition, an increase in self-respect was noted, but in particular many of the squatters felt a sense of power as others who had been in the shelter system began to view them as having access to power, at being able to help them find housing. This felt sense of power translated into a sense of collective responsibility for other homeless. Jim mentioned, "I feel like we're responsible to reach back and grab those that can't help themselves. Now I go some places and see some guys who knew that I was a part of the hut dwellers and the media thing and they say, 'Hey, Jim! Can I get a place? Tell me what to do.'" With the new found attention and the willingness of the city to negotiate for the huts Jim held out for three additional days:

> I talked to the commissioner eye to eye. He and I had words, Daniel Alvarez from the city of Chicago Department of Human Services. He came in with the contract

that he wanted me to sign and I was the only hut dweller around there. I was really adhering to what he wanted and he was tired and wanted me to get together with the other guys who were already housed. So, he approached me and wanted me to sign a waiver that I was giving my hut to the city of Chicago to do whatever they wanted with it and I disagreed with that. And I told him to re-write that because I felt that the hut was my property and I want to know where my hut is that. I may want to donate to whoever I want it donated to. He said he couldn't do that and I said I'm not leaving. I told him to get off my land! I had words like that and I knew it was hard for him to understand a person's basic needs, a person's own ability to know what he was dealing with, which was an emergency basis. It was something very personal and private and he just wanted me to throw it away. It was like this man, . . . this . . . authority is not even listening to me. He wanted me to sign the papers and just get off the land and I wasn't goin' for that. I told him that sense he had that type of attitude that I was going to stay three more days. I told him I would give him the decision in three more days what I was gonna do with my hut. So we cost the city some money.

The ability to delay the city of Chicago for three days was in fact a real demonstration of power for those in the encampments. Others described the encampment as "educational" with a wide variety of ethnic, racial, and religious groupings visiting the encampment to lend their support. The squatters thought that this helped to broaden their perspective. As Tim mentioned, "we learned new things. Sometimes people would come down there and give us certain issues to talk about. Not only did we talk about our needs but about everbody's." One member of the camp was able to secure his old job when his employer read about the encampment in the local newspaper. Mutual support was mentioned by all as one of the gains of the encampment. One squatter said that it taught him the "will to live." He said:

I was about ready to commit suicide. These guys told me there would be better days. They kept on trying and they told me not to worry about it and that something would happen. We got a place where we can hide and we got people that are helping us. I gave up on the matter. But they told me don't give up and that's why I'm here.

Friendship, comradeship and a sense of solidarity were all mentioned as key benefits for the squatters. As a result of their organizing they were able to attract city attention that further confirmed the viability for collective empowerment. One squatter said that after moving from a six-bedroom unit to a shelter to a hut he had a greater appreciation for living space: "I get respect for a home. I used to take it for granted. No more." Another squatter who had just been released from prison mentioned that working with the encampment had revealed a way to act which could accomplish the same ends without violent action:

> I respect people like I've always respected them but with a little bit more detail. If you piss me off I'm gonna go get the police. I ain't gonna bust your head. I'm gonna get the police and file a complaint against you. I'm gonna lock you up.

So, you learned that from being in the encampments?

> Oh, yes because I didn't have nothing. Now I have something. I have a lease. For example, if you bust my window I'm gonna get the police and I'm gonna file charges against you. I'm gonna make you pay for the window and I'm gonna get the police to make sure you don't come around the house no more.

What appears to have been gained in addition to respect and feelings of self-worth is a new faith in the possibility of organizing for change. The expansion of the possibilities for change resulted from the employment of disruptive, non-normative tactics through squatting. As Piven and Cloward point out, for poor people who lack the resources of middle-class organizations, disruption may be the only way to precipitate change (Piven & Cloward 1992, 1977). However, the effects of such disruptions are not limited to established institutions, but directly affect the perception of future possibilities for change within poor populations. This hope for change combined with the direct practical experience of squatting, and developing organizational skills, seems to be one of the lasting benefits of the encampment. Perhaps Jim says it best:

> I've gained insight into this homeless issue. I understand it a little better than I did in the past based upon organizing ourselves with the group. I've learned that a lot of people do care about the homeless. I was surprised that we had a lot of support from people in suburbs. I've learned that a lot of people watch the news, man! I've learned that you can achieve a lot once you put your heads together toward a common goal. Any person trying to accomplish any kind of task alone is gonna be hard. Two heads are better than one. We achieved a lot because we came together and we spoke up for ourselves. And we asked ourselves what we want and how each other feel. We organized. And I know that I have learned a skill. And that skill is an organizational skill.[36]

Notes

1. This is an expanded version of a paper delivered to the 1994 Midwest Sociological Association Meetings, St. Louis, Missouri. A final draft was presented to Wayne, one of the former members of the homeless encampment for discussion with the other members and with myself over the content and form of the research. The following footnoted comments by him are the result of a two hour

followup interview. His views reflect most of those in the encampment. This style of presenting the text and commentary on the text by the subjects investigated is in keeping with the spirit of critical ethnography (Hammersley 1992; Thomas 1993), critical pedagogy and dialogic research (Aronowitz and Giroux 1991, 114–35, 157–84; Giroux 1888, 1991) and Friere (1973, 1978). It also recognizes that the authority of the ethnographic text is never complete (Clifford 1988; Clifford and Marcus 1986), but subject to different interpretations depending upon one's authoritative position. Elliot Liebow in his new book about homeless women, *Tell Them Who I Am* (1993), also uses this method to generate a dialogue with the reader. While this is not a complete collaborative work between myself and the men I worked with I have attempted to provide for a voice about the text. See also the work of Mishler (1986, 117–35). This is an attempt to reinsert the authority of the subject back into the text by creating a dialogue between the subject and text through which the reader can participate.

2. WAYNE: There was approximately twenty-two huts in all, total. . . . That was the total amount. We didn't tell them everyone. There was some hidden farther north that we didn't tell nobody about. The total amount of people housed right here was something like fifty, forty-five, forty-seven.

3. In Rappaport's (1984) understanding of empowerment, "empowerment is viewed as a process: the mechanism by which people, organizations, and communities gain mastery over their own lives" (1984, 3). However, the vagueness of this definition allows for a multiplicity of interpretations which dilute the concept's analytical qualities. If empowerment does not include an analysis of social power, the conditions which generate the need for individual empowerment in the first instance will not be addressed.

     Kieffer (1984, 9) reduces empowerment to "a necessarily long-term process of adult learning and development." This technical definition ignores larger social and political issues. However, it is important to understand that "feeling more powerful" as opposed to "being more powerful" may be a necessary first step in altering not only one's own position, but also that of others in society. As Keiffer (1984) says, "the fundamental empowering transformation, then, is in the transition from sense of self as helpless victim to acceptance of self as assertive and efficacious citizen" (p. 32). This individualized success model of empowerment fails not because it is unimportant to overcome feelings of powerlessness, but because it does not go far enough in analyzing the real structural constraints on everyday life and because it lacks an ethical basis in principles of social justice. In Irma Serrano-Garcia's (1984) analysis of empowerment, through a community development experience in Puerto Rico, this limitation becomes evident. Empowerment was just another ideological illusion masking the impact of cultural colonization by the United States. While people gained greater control over their lives, that control did not translate into a critical ideology based upon social justice. Hence, individual empowerment that accepts status quo goals of individual success at the expense of the social, sustained inequality, individualism, and private over social property reproduces the very inequality which creates the need for empowerment in the first place. Relationships of property and power are not challenged. Collective empowerment, as I am using it here, refers to the advancement of a group or class of individuals through collective action, in which collective identities are established, if only for a short time based upon a project which challenges established relationships of power, property, and space.

4. The higher figure of fifty was given to us by Wayne after all the interviews were completed. It was very difficult to develop an accurate count since people moved

through the huts on a frequent basis, some staying for as little as a few days, others for months.

5. Metra had written the Mayor. Metra, and then Old Milwaukee, the owner of the property, sent a letter to the Mayor's office and he came down and okayed it to us in person.

6. And you could add, they were clearly visible from the Metra trains. Yeah, because they started slowing them down, even stopping them, and the conductors would show everybody where there're at. Cause' a lot of people did see them, and they would be standing up in the windows looking for them. And that's when they started slowing the trains down, so they could show them exactly where they were at.

7. Oh, yeah. Cause' then they label everybody. Anytime time you go to a shelter and you got to sit up and take a breathalizer test and you tell somebody you don't drink, and you don't have it on your breath, and you are letting them know I'm not an alcoholic, and I have never been one, and they still say you got to take the test, and the other fact is that it's unsanitary. . . . You can't label everybody because one person is an alcoholic and you know it.

8. That came about when the Mad Housers themselves went down to City Hall and tried to have a meeting with Commissioner Alvarez. We knew something like that was going to happen because of the conflict with _____ tell'n the other guys "we could tell them for ourselves." All of as are together. This is what I was telling them. And everybody had to say what they want, where they want to live, and all that. But, we didn't want nobody from the Mad Housers. We made that clear from the jump street - we was going to do our own negotiating. We told them we wanted you to be around for the support, that was the main thing. And if we needed any technical assistance whatsoever then we would cover you all. Cause' as long as your're there we could ask you. But, not to negotiate the meeting itself. We was going to do that. . . . This was something they tried to do (Mad Housers meeting with the Commissioner) and then the Commissioner came to us and said, "Well I've been negotiating.. I been talking to the wrong people all the time." I said yeah, Because whatever you negotiate with them is not going to mean anything. You got to come down here and talk with the people who this is going to effect. . . . You get people on the outside that don't know better, that don't know exactly what's going on. . . . _____ and all of them didn't know exactly what was happening.

   We knew that the owner of the property we was on said it's okay; "You got these four [huts] here, but don't put anymore on it." Cause' he was checking out everything in the paper everyday . . . The owner of the property came down to see us. And the Mad Housers went and put huts on one side of the other end down there . . . Kedzie Bridge . . . One side was okay, but on the opposite side they put some huts that was too close to some kind of butane tank or something and the railroad department said that's too dangerous for those guys to be here.

9. Come on! I mean, clear the area of debris? All that time we was down there we cleaned up more than the city did. I mean, we had people come'n down there trying to dump on our property, so we had to run'em off. We had the city streetsweeper came down there and dump some stuff. . . . [the huts] those were our cribs.

10. The purpose of these degradation ceremonies, aside from conveying a lowered social status, is to separate out the deserving from the undeserving homeless. Those who obey are deserving. Those who do not are undeserving. An extension

of this arrangement within the professions is what Estroff (1985) terms "medicalizing the margins." Whether or not one deserves attention is dependent upon one being perceived as "ill." Evidence of "illness" is produced through disorderly appearance or behavior. For those homeless who do not appear ill or disorderly the label of undeserving may well be applied. In addition, as Katz (1989) points out because of societal expectations of women as nurturers and mothers, homeless families, will receive a greater degree of public sympathy, the status of deserving, versus young single males, who are labeled as recalcitrant.

11. Some people don't really know how to run a shelter. . . . And then when you have a lot of people that are volunteer staff, as far as like other homeless individuals, who tend to forget that they are still homeless, but they're working in the shelter, and the only difference is you get better clothing, better food to eat, but your still homeless, you're still living in the shelter, they seem to forget. It's like homeless rejecting homeless.

    They have volunteers in there who don't really know what's happening with people. See they don't understand like when they ask for another spoonful of food. Maybe they want another one. And they don't understand that because they got to tell them well now we can't really give you anymore. Well you know they going to throw [the food]. What ther'e going to do with all this extra food is trash it, cause they can't keep it.

12. A lot of people feel that way because of the gangs and the lack of security. Whether or not, there is a lot of shelters that are not secure.

13. And then you have shelters which do not have grievance committees. Like, if you got a complaint against somebody, to where it almost means you get physical with you and with somebody on staff. If you don't have nobody actually to complain to then it's your word against him and if you don't like it, don't come in. Or they might have authority where you can't come in no more because they said so because of what you did, you argued with him so he could say you can't come in, this is the reason why you can't come in, and they (shelter staff) will follow with him. Grievance committees should be in all shelters, I think. And there should be some homeless people on it.

14. They was talk'n about the Cook County sheriff guys over there. They something else. They don't want to have nothing to do with you, they don't want to touch you, don't want to shake your hand, don't barely want to speak. Had two of them like that. They really had a bad, bad attitude.

15. People get their mail at the shelters. That's usually an SSI check. People should come to them or on the intercom system, not announce anything about checks and tell them to come to the office. And do that behind closed doors. Not hand them a check in front at the window. They need to work out a system were people getting mail like that as far as checks, that, that don't be done in the open where everybody know's your business. . . . If it's on the first of the month, all the SSI checks, and you got twenty or thirty people coming to pick up checks, that shouldn't be done while everybody else is around. I seen people get robbed as soon as they get their checks. Sometime outside the shelter, they wait until they go in the shelter, wait until they comeback down. I see individuals get robbed as soon as they step out of the currency exchange. They wait until they cash the checks. They follow them. You don't have no security once you leave the shelter with you check.

16. Some of them may have corrected that by now, especially some of the West Side shelters.

17. I've been in shelters where you didn't get in the shower until eleven o'clock at

night.

18. Well they have rules. I don't think they should throw nobody on the street because he's drunk. I think there should be an alternate plan for that. I mean, if the man is that drunk they should make the necessary phone calls or the connections to get this man where he can detox. But, not send him back on the street when it's ten to fifteen below zero. . . . And he'll be one of the guys found in the morning dead somewhere because they didn't, wouldn't let him in because he had alcohol. There's got to be an alternate for that as well.

19. In a random sampling of 150 homeless persons in Birmingham, Alabama by La Gory, Ritchey and Mullis (1989) it was discovered that extensive networks of friends, relatives, confidants, and acquaintances existed among the population, although these relationships appeared to have only modest impact on helping one out of their situation.

20. A big difference. You have your own control. You have control on your life, yourself. You don't have people telling you what to do, when to do it, how to do it. Whereas, in the shelter it was difficult for me to get at the day labor in time so I could be one of the first chosen to go out to work. When'n the shelters, you cannot get up until this time. For they have a rule, like the Pacific Garden Mission, you can't leave out of that shelter until five o'clock. Were use to getting up at four in order to get coffee, get some breakfast before day labor actually opens. If they got a rule where you can't leave till five, you can't leave till five. And the doors are locked at the Pacific Garden Mission and an alarm system turned on. You can't leave out of there until five . . . no matter how early you have to leave to go to work. What happens is people won't stay at that shelter. They will go to another one or like me, stay outside.

21. I was there. They had young white kids, 17, 18, 19. We go to this day labor all damn year long and were look'n at these 17, 18, 19 year old white kids from Bridgeport being supervisors over us. Now none of us have the jobs yet but were standing out here, and they got us like in a damn corral with a fence all around. And this is where we have to stand like cattle waiting on them to call our names . . . We had told a lot of people, we brought a lot of people down there, and then we get there, and waiting and waiting over an hour, and don't get the jobs. That's what ticked everybody off. Then you got people that did get the jobs. Ther'e being supervised by the young kids. It's bad enough having the young kids as supervisor, but then to be talked down to, to be talked down to in that tone of voice, "You got to come over here and you got to always be in sight where I can see you, and all that." If the man is doing his job what do you care? It don't make a difference whether you see him or not. If you're his supervisor you're supposed to know where he is at anyhow.

22. And that's how they treat you. Like you was nothing.

23. Because we got respect there [the encampment], see. We got respect from the Metra police, the City police. We got respect from the community business people. They helped us out. They supported what we was doing.
    When people seen the way we was keeping the whole area clean, I mean we didn't have to be out there on the railroad tracks chopping weeds down they got people that do that, they get paid for that. We was doing that, was cleaning up the whole area. People were looking at that, and some of the people in the community, the business community was bringing us shovels, garbage bags to put it in. And they would tell us put it over here at this dumpster.

24. Hey, where's the duck? You didn't mention the duck! The pair of ducks. Remember we talked about that female duck that was in the pool of water for so long.

And all of a sudden we got up one morning and this duck was in this little pool of water like a pond from the rain and that duck wouldn't leave for nothn'. So we was taking food and stuff, everyday that duck would be there. Finally a male duck came and then they left. That's when that duck left. That duck just sit there like she knew she wait'n on somebody to come. We had quite a few different kind of birds over there, robins, woodpeckers, plenty of finches, they woke you up in the morning.

25. Tranquility City was a beautiful place . . . It's like peaceful, not a care in the world, nobody's bothering you, we listen to the radio, we listen to our gospel station, and you just kick back. And somebody walk up, and you ask them, "you want a cold drink?" . . . Come on sit down for a little while. It was something I haven't seen in a long time. I seen this done in the country when people would be walking down the road, for long walks to get somewhere. And then they stop and wipe the sweat, and then, you'll see this one house and somebody come'n out with a pitcher of water or something and invite you to sit under the shade trees. That's what made me thought about Tranquility City. You hardly see that anymore.

26. That's the attitude at first with a lot of guys. But, I told them as you can see, don't nobody want to bother you. The drugs, its not just public housing that's has drugs, you have to remember that. You have other neighborhoods, just regular neighborhoods. They have drugs in them. They have a worse problem than over here. Because, when they got here this is what they seen. And this wasn't happening in the huts. It was a shock.
If you go from the huts, and you know how peaceful and quiet it was there, and you go over to Rockwell and all of a sudden somebody break out shooting, and No, I don't want to stay here. Immediate panic set in, no, no, no. . . . You think about the huts and you think about when you first went in this place and you say, "Damn I had better security with the fellows than this." It's a good point. And you say, I think I'm going to stay in my hut. But, that was Rockwell Gardens.

27. When they see the weak ones. They size you up. You can't show them that your weak. You can't show that side.

28. We networked with everybody around there. The bars. We had a bar on the corner, two bars on opposite sides of each other. They let us put flyers in and everything. Anytime we need anything, as far as calling people, they would make that arrangement and do it themselves.

29. We had our little group sit downs. You know, nice day, get under the trees, sit down and discuss it. You know a lot of people would tell what happened to them. How they was doing, what they had, what they lost—and we even had some of the people crying while they was talking about it. And they would get up and want to go away, and we would tell them we support what you are doing. Man, you got friends here. You don't have to leave and be ashamed of crying, because everybody cries. We let them know we're there for you. We got to stick together.

30. We already had talked about that and discussed that [before the Mayor's decision to remove the huts]. We already said that this was not just about us. We're talkn' about over 60,000 people homeless. Me, _____ and _____ already decided that. It was not just going to be about us and them, we leave and that's it. That's why we wanted to be the last people to leave. That decision was made among us three, that we was going to be there until the end no matter what. Then we discussed with all the other guys. We held a meeting, told them what we was going to do and wanted to know their views, how they felt about it, and what they think about joining in on it. Because, they going to try to divide us when push comes to

shove. So everybody needs to be aware that they have their own choices of what it is they want to do.

31. Then the panhandling thing. They [those living under Kedzie Bridge] wanted to come down on our end because of all the traffic . . . and panhandle down there. See, we didn't want to start that except'n money thing. We didn't. Cause' we know people's going to come down there and try and manipulate one of us or all of us against each other with any kind of means to get us to fight among each other. And that's one way to do it. Because, if somebody comes on one end with all this money, and that happened on that end by the way, and give it to one individual and don't tell the other ones, and that person that gave it to them tells them to split it with everybody, and if they see this person again and they tell him, it could bring up problems. We don't want people to feel that the only reason why they have to come down there is to make sure you bring us money. We didn't want no money. If you want to use money in that sense, don't give it to us, get something with it, things that we need. All of the guys were around and then they understood why we didn't want to panhandle and stuff.

These guys didn't know no better because they were still in that rut. They were used to panhandling on Lower Wacker and that had to change. It took awhile for a lot of people to get used to their places. Some of the guys when they stepped in their doors were crying, like babies, they couldn't believe they actually had their own place finally.

32. That's right. That's when we had to tell them no, no, no you made a mistake now.

33. That's because the ones that wanted the Mad Housers to represent them didn't know exactly what was going on with the negotiations. They were not fully aware of everything that was involved. . . . The Mad Housers did not know all of the details that were involved. We sat down, pages and pages writing this stuff up.

34. The attitude was more focused on the hut than the human aspect of it. To us it wasn't about just a piece of wood. Your dealing with a person, as a human being with emotions.

35. Down there at the huts it made everybody realize what was going on. Politically wise—were looking, some shacks, man, with paint cans for heaters. Were not bothering anybody, and were not on city property in the first place . . . and were not terrorizing the neighborhood or anything and all of a sudden the City is like sending out the war party after us. And all the head leaders. Now what the hell is all the head leaders coming? The Commissioner from Streets and Sands, the Commissioner for Buildings and Codes, the Supervisor of the park district. All of the head people, none of the understudies. That was definitely politics then, when we start see all of these people come down to a group of homeless people. Please! . . . Politically this was a big ass problem for [Mayor] Daley . . . He knew we meant what we said. He knew we weren't leaving without a fight. Anybody touch these huts can get ready for a physical confrontation.

36. This really gave everybody a skill, organizing people together, a sense of joining forces, getting teamwork. . . . We all came together in the final phase. Were still together. I would hope people learn something from this, I know I learned a lot.

References

Aronowitz, S. and H. A. Giroux (1991). *Postmodern Education: Politics, Culture & Social Criticism.* Minneapolis, MN: University of Minnesota Press.

City of Chicago (1994). *Comprehensive Housing Affordability Strategy.* City of Chicago, Chicago, Illinois.

Clifford, J. (1988). *The Predicament of Culture: Twentieth-Century Ethnography, Literature, and Art.* Cambridge, MA: Harvard University Press.

Clifford, J. and G. E. Marcus, eds. (1986). *Writing Culture: The Poetics and Politics of Ethnography.* Berkeley, CA: University of California Press.

Estroff, S. E. (1985). "Medicalizing the Margins: On Being Disgraced, Disordered, and Deserving." *Psychosocial Rehabilitation Journal* 8:34–39.

Foucault, M. (1986). "Of Other Space." *Diacritics.* Spring:22–27.

Friere, P. (1973). *Pedagogy of the Oppressed.* New York: Seabury.

Friere, P. (1978). *Education for Critical Consciousness.* New York: Seabury.

Garfinkel, H. (1956). "Conditions of Successful Degradation Ceremonies." *American Journal of Sociology* 61:240–44.

Giroux, H. A. (1988). *Schooling and the Struggle for Public Life: Critical Pedagogy in the Modern Age.* Minneapolis, MN.: University of Minnesota Press.

Giroux, H. A. (1991). *Border Crossings: Cultural Workers and the Politics of Education.* New York: Routledge.

Goffman, E. (1963). *Behavior in Public Places: Notes on the Social Organization of Gatherings.* New York: Free Press.

Hammersley, M. (1992). *What's Wrong with Ethnography.* New York: Routledge.

Hoch, C. and R. Slayton (1989). *New Homeless and Old: Community and the Skid Row Hotel.* Philadelphia: Temple University Press.

Homeless Refuse to go on CHA Tour (1992). *Chicago Tribune,* June 2, Sec.2, pg.3.

Kasinitz, P. (1986). "Gentrification and Homelessness: The Single Room Occupant and the Inner City Revival. In *Housing the Homeless,* edited by J. Erickson and C. Wilhelm, 241–52. New Brunswick, NJ: Center for Urban Policy Research.

Katz, M. B. (1989). *The Undeserving Poor: From the War on Poverty to the War on Welfare.* NY: Pantheon Books.

Kieffer, C. (1984). "Citizen Empowerment: A Developmental Perspective. In *Studies in Empowerment: Steps Towards Understanding and Action,* edited by J. Rappaport and R. Hess, 9–23. New York: Hayworth Press.

La Gory, M., F. Ritchey, and J. Mullis (1989). Homelessness and Affiliation. Paper given at the Eighty-Fourth Annual American Sociological Association Conference, San Francisco, CA.

Liebow, L. (1993). *Tell Them Who I Am: The Lives of Homeless Women.* New York: Free Press.

Marcuse, P. (1989). "Gentrification, Homelessness, and the Work Process." *Housing Studies* 4:211–20.

Melucci, A. (1989). *Nomads of the Present: Social Movements and Individual Needs in Contemporary Society.* Philadelphia, PA: Temple University Press.

Melucci, A. (1988). "Getting Involved: Identity and Mobilization in Social Movements." *International Social Movement Research* 1:329–48.

Mishler, E. (1986). *Research Interviewing.* Cambridge, MA: Harvard University Press

Piven, F. F. and R. Cloward (1992). "Normalizing Collective Protest." In *Frontiers in Social Movement Theory,* edited by A. D. Morris and C. M. Mueller, 301–25 New Haven, CT.: Yale University Press.

Piven, F. F. and R. Cloward (1977). *Poor People's Movements: Why They Succeed, How They Fail.* New York: Pantheon.

Rappaport, J. and R. Hess (1984). *Studies in Empowerment: Steps Towards Understanding and Action.* New York: Hayworth Press.

Robertson, M. (1991). "Interpreting Homelessness: The Influence of Professional and

Non-Professional Service Providers." *Urban Anthropology,* 20:141–53.

Ropers, R. H. (1988). *The Invisible Homeless: A New Urban Ecology.* New York: Insight Books.

Rosenthal, R. (1989). "Worlds Within Worlds: The Lives of Homeless People in Context." Paper presented at the Eighty-Fourth Annual American Sociological Association Conference, San Francisco, CA.

Rosenthal, R. (1991). "Straighter from the Source: Alternative Methods of Researching Homelessness." *Urban Anthropology* 20:109–26.

Rosenthal, R. (1994). *Homeless in Paradise: A Map of the Terrain.* Philadelphia: Temple University Press.

Rossi, P. (1989). *Down and Out in America: The Origins of Homelessness.* Chicago: University of Chicago Press.

Ruddick, S. (1990). "Heterotopias of the Homeless: Strategies and Tactics of Placemaking in Los Angeles." *Strategies* 3:184–201.

Serrano-Garcia, I. (1984). "The Illusion of Empowerment: Community Development Within a Colonial Context." In *Studies in Empowerment: Steps Towards Understanding and Action,* edited by J. Rappaport and R. Hess, 173–200. New York: Hayworth.

Smith, Z. N. (1992). "Homeless huts draw support from City Hall to living room." *Chicago Sun-Times,* February 5, pg.4.

Smith, Z. N. (1992a). "City no longer tolerates homeless huts." *Chicago Sun-Times,* May 21, pg.3,77.

Smith, Z. N. (1992b). "Daley decision hits homeless where they live." *Chicago Sun-Times,* May 22, pg.4.

Smith, Z. N. (1992c). "Huts periled by proposal for 'urban Ravinia.'" *Chicago Sun-Times,* June 4, pg.6.

Smith, Z. N. (1992d). "City take 7 homeless huts." *Chicago Sun-Times,* June 11, pg.5.

Snow, D. A. and L. Anderson (1993). *Down on Their Luck: A Study of Homeless Street People.* Berkeley: University of California Press.

Stein, S. (1992). "West Loop shelters feeling pressure as gentrification knocks." *Chicago Tribune,* November 23, Sec. 2, pg.5.

Thomas, K. and P. A. Wright (1990). *An Assessment of Single Room Occupancy (SRO) Hotels in the South Loop.* Technical Report 2–90. The Nathalie P. Voorhees Center for Neighborhood and Community Improvement. Chicago, Illinois.

Thorn, J. (1993). "Doing Critical Ethnography." *Qualitative research methods series #26.* Newbury Park, CA: Sage.

Thorton, J. (1992). "City searches for a compromise on eliminating homeless huts." *Chicago Tribune,* May 27, Pg.2, Sec.2.

Timmer, D. A. (1988, November). "Homelessness as Deviance: The Ideology of the Shelter." *Free Inquiry in Creative Sociology,* 16:163–70.

Wagner, D. (1993). *Checkerboard Square: Culture and Resistance in a Homeless Community.* Boulder, CO: Westview.

Wagner, D., and M. B. Cohen (1991). "The Power of the People: Homeless Protesters in the Aftermath of Social Movement Participation." *Social Problems* 38:543–61.

3

Private Redevelopment and the Changing Forms of Displacement in the East Village of New York

Christopher Mele

The chaos that once characterized street life on a stretch of Avenue C in New York's East Village is now muted. The unlicensed elderly Latino street vendors of household goods—from black-and-white televisions to kitchen utensils—have moved on; the heckling of the more desperate drug users by teenagers seems less frequent; the graffiti-scarred bricks of a five-story apartment building have been painted over, and all the units inside have been renovated by its latest private developer. Finally, the torched shells of three five-story tenements have been reconstructed under a community-sponsored alternative housing plan and are once again occupied by low and middle-income tenants. Although this description depicts a harmonious image of a mixed land-use neighborhood, it conceals more than a decade of controversy and struggle between private developers, the state, and residents over residential displacement and the gentrification of what was once one of the few remaining low-rent districts in Lower Manhattan, the East Village.

In July of 1986, the sixteen-story landmark Christodora House, located one block west of Avenue C, reopened with its units newly renovated as luxury condominiums. It was a momentous occasion in East Village history for at least two sets of important local actors. For developers, it was the plunder of a hard-fought battle to bring the neighborhood into the fold of the 1980s Manhattan housing market of expensive luxury units. The prize was significant. Located in the heart of the "untamed" East Village on the east side of Tompkins Square Park, the Christodora's many past uses read like a larger history of the Lower East Side. It was constructed in 1928 as a settlement house, left vacant for most of the 1940s and 1950s, partially let out to the Black Panthers in the 1960s, sold by the city to a real estate developer in 1975, and resold (flipped) twice before finally being renovated (Gordon, 1994). For the most optimistic of the city's real estate community, the Christodora was the flagship for their efforts to displace the low-income image of the East Village (*Real Estate Newsletter*, 1985).

For a loosely connected group of residents, including squatters, ex-hippies, community activists, and housing advocates, the reopening of the Christodora was a line drawn in the sand. The building—more precisely, its symbolism—crystallized the antigentrification movement. The Christodora gave the "enemy" (developers) a name and an address that could be used to rally the troops at antigentrification demonstrations, conjure up negative images of real estate displacement and colonization at community board meetings, and to vent anger about "yuppie" incursions into the last haven in Manhattan unspoiled by 1980s greed and materialism.

The relative quiet in the East Village of the 1990s is less a compromise between developers, the state, and residents than a deadlock over the direction of neighborhood change (Abu-Lughod et al., 1994). Indeed, as I hope to show in this article, the conflict between developers and low-income residents is far from over; only the tactics have changed. Like other centrally located inner city neighborhoods of larger North American cities in the late 1970s and 1980s, speculators, individual landlords and developers, with incentives and subsidies from the state, sought to profit from the displacement of low-income households and the subsequent transformation of land use for middle- and high-income residents. Unlike many other communities undergoing similar transformations, however, the restructuring of the East Village was more pronounced and contested (Mele 1993). Because the East Village was home to a substantial community of low-income and mostly Latino residents with *de jure* rental protection, displacement was never a foregone conclusion of the massive redevelopment efforts financed by real estate capitalists. Instead, redevelopment proceeded slowly as a heated turf war pitting the inventiveness of real estate capitalists against the limited resources of residents who were determined to carve out a space for resistance to displacement. Consequently, the story of residential displacement in the East Village from the early 1980s to the present has much to reveal about the political economy of neighborhood change and community response and resistance to it.

Changes in the dominant means of displacing low-income tenants in the East Village have progressed from the harassment and eviction of individual residents in the 1980s to the recent attempt by developers to appropriate and alter the community's self-styled identity for profitable ends. In this article I analyze the evolution of these various strategies for the purpose of redefining and expanding the concept of residential displacement as a dynamic and often untidy process, rather than as a fixed or static outcome of gentrification. Within an urban political economy framework, I analyze the progression from one form of displacement to another as a flexible response to challenges to the real estate agenda of transforming land use to "better and higher uses." Alongside a political economic explanation, I employ an ethnographic approach that brings a more detailed and applied dimension to understanding displacement and that smoothes some of rougher "functionalist" edges of political economy (Gottdiener 1985, chapter 3). I present ethnographic evidence to specify how the different strategies of displacement were played out, transformed, and resisted in the apartment buildings and streets of the East Village. The ethnographic material presented in this paper is a result of three years residence in several transitional gentrifying buildings in the far-eastern section of the neighborhood (Loisaida), where real estate capitalists' attempts to reclaim and transform these blocks and neighborhood resistance were intense.[1]

From observations and interviews with tenants, community activists, landlords, and developers, I have compiled a portrait of real estate activities and strategies and resistance to them. From conversations with real estate agents and owners I learned of the changes in techniques to move out low-income residents and replace them with higher rent-paying tenants. From my neighbors, I learned the mechanics of displacement pressures and ways of circumventing them, why some residents moved away and why others felt hopelessly trapped. As I hope to show in this paper, this material is not anecdotal or "local color," but integral to bettering our understanding of the political economy of displacement and neighborhood restructuring in at least two ways. First, the use of ethnography helps reduce the distance between political economic analysis of displacement (in which the removal of tenants facilitates capital accumulation) and the complexity of displacement as worked out in everyday urban life. Second, ethnographic materials provide us a clearer picture of agency, power, and resistance to move beyond an understanding of displacement as an unexpressed consequence of redevelopment.

Displacement and Urban Sociology

When urban sociologists speak of displacement they are typically referring to the net result of the involuntary migration of incumbent poor residents out of downtown neighborhoods as a result of urban restructuring. Scholarly interest in the subject began in the late 1970s and early 1980s when the built environments of inner city neighborhoods in several larger U.S. cities were being transformed by real estate capital investment (gentrification). Some of the earliest studies of displacement, including the first clear definition of the concept (Grier and Grier 1978), were commissioned by the U.S. Department of Housing and Urban Development (HUD) (Weiler 1978; U.S. Department of Housing and Urban Development 1979 and 1981). The HUD-commissioned studies set out to verify the existence of displacement and to determine how much, if any, displacement had occurred as a result of revitalization by private developers. More important than their findings was the influence of these studies on the way in which displacement continues to be discussed and analyzed. The methodology of displacement studies borrows heavily from evaluation research. Studies are typically designed as comparisons of demographic "snapshots" taken before the onset of neighborhood upgrading and after with only cursory treatment given to the process of *displacing* (Cincin-Sain 1980).

Both traditional and critical urban sociologists have treated displacement as an outcome of a process of neighborhood transformation. Proponents of a consumer market explanation of neighborhood revitalization viewed displacement as an unfortunate, yet "natural" consequence of the dynamics of the housing market (Lee and Hodge 1984: 141–42). Since data had consistently shown high levels of residential mobility for poor renters in inner city neighborhoods, analyses proved inconclusive in determining whether what appeared as gentrification-caused displacement was, in actuality, frequent voluntary mobility (Sumka 1979; Palen and London 1984, 260-63). Analyses by critical urban sociologists contradicted the view of displacement as epiphenomenal or accidental to the process of revitalization (Hartman 1979a and 1979b). Instead, they considered involuntary outmigration of the poor, the elderly, and minorities as a negative structural outcome of capital accumulation (Marcuse 1985; Smith 1988, 147; Feagin and Parker 1990, chapter 5) or a "vicious side-effect" (Goldfield 1980) of profit-driven urban restructuring.

The tendency toward analysis of displacement as a consequence of urban change reduces the concept to a static one and disguises the versatile ways displacement is played out by real estate capitalists and resisted by threatened residents. The following sections offer an analysis of how the versatility of the displacement process was instrumental to the restructuring of the East Village. Several patterns emerge. First, the means of displacing low-income tenants were constantly modified. Existing tactics were either effectively challenged by residents or made obsolete by new opportunities, such as state development incentives. The strategies employed by developers over time to displace residents ranged in degree of compulsion, from harassing and evicting tenants to coopting and marketing the neighborhood's "bohemian" image. Finally, as evidence form ethnographic work demonstrates, displacement was not a passive outcome of urban restructuring, but a contest between residents and developers. Resistance to redevelopment mounted by residents has consistently forced realtors to revise their displacement strategies.

The Political Economy of Residential Change in the East Village

The area of lower Manhattan known since the 1960s as the East Village is located in the historic working-class district of the Lower East Side. Its boundaries are from south to north, Houston Street to 14th Street and from west to east, Third Avenue to FDR Drive. Its recognition as a distinct enclave follows a historical trend of the emergence and decline of resident quarters within the larger Lower East Side. During the nineteenth century, successive waves of European immigrants carved out enclaves that reflected their ethnic heritage. In the 1860s, the German enclave, Kleinedeutschland, was founded followed by the Jewish and Italian quarters in the early 1900s. These small entities were transformed within decades and eventually vanished as their cohort of residents voluntarily relocated to better neighborhoods only to be replaced by newcomers of different ethnic backgrounds. Today, the Lower East Side, south of Houston Street, remains continuously transformed by immigration from Asia, Central and South America, and the Caribbean. In the East Village to the north, Puerto Rican migrants established the last ethnic enclave of Loisaida in the 1950-60s.

Amidst more than a century of continuous residential change, one significant continuity—the role of housing producers—has endured. Historically the residents of the Lower East Side have been renters, not homeowners. Ownership of the majority of tenement buildings has been through absentee landlords. Most properties, therefore, have been investments and income-generating rental properties. Consequently, the role of real estate capitalists—speculators, landlords, developers— has been tightly interwoven into the fabric of Lower East Side history and has figured prominently in the course of neighborhood change.

The most recent designation, "East Village," reflects the influence of real estate actors. Following World War II, public housing projects dominated the blocks bordering the East River, especially along the southeastern Lower East Side. Local realtors sought to distance their adjacent rental housing from these "unprofitable" zones and coined the "East Village" to describe the area from 14th Street to Houston and the Bowery to First Avenue. By carving out the East Village from the Lower East Side, landlords hoped to mimic the West Village's profitable trajectory of development from a bohemian colony to an upper-middle class enclave. Those aspirations were tempered, however, by New York's stagnant economy and fiscal crisis in the 1970s. Many landlords sought short-term profits through disinvesting then abandoning their holdings.

Several factors converged in the 1980s to provide a new impetus for private redevelopment in what real estate investors considered the last "residual housing market south of Central Park."[2]

First, changes in New York City's political economy fostered opportunities for real estate capitalists to create newer and "higher" uses out of working-class housing in centrally located low-income and mostly minority neighborhoods. New York's economic transformation was characterized by growth in global services industries on one hand and an increase in downgraded manufacturing on the other (Sassen 1991).

The shift toward corporate finance, insurance, and producer services, which took off in the mid-1970s, created new well-paying employment opportunities for professionals in Manhattan and a subsequent conversion of middle-class rental apartments into luxury housing. Investments in converting middle-class rental apartments into more expensive condominiums and cooperatives became increasingly lucrative for land owners. This, in turn, limited the stock of affordable rental housing and fed the demand for newly renovated and affordable (but not low-income) units in areas, such as the East Village and the West Side's Hell's Kitchen (reinvented as Clinton), that were formerly deemed unmarketable. Speculators saw the potential for profit in redeveloping the East Village's housing market for white-collar workers in the nearby Wall Street and Midtown office districts. Extensive upper-middle class development of adjacent neighborhoods, such as SoHo in Lower Manhattan, was well under way by the early 1980s (Zukin 1982). Finally, the housing disinvestment of the 1970s left East Village land prices extremely low compared to Manhattan land values.

In the ensuing decade, restructuring led to the displacement of low-income residents. As realtors invested in the East Village, residents of the predominantly Latino community of Loisaida have been subjected to a variety of forms of residential displacement. In DeGiovanni's 1987 study of displacement pressures on the Lower East Side, Latinos constituted more than a third of the total population of outmigrants. According to census figures, Latino residents dropped 14.5 percent in their share of the total East Village population between 1980 and 1990, whereas for all of Manhattan, Latinos increased 13.2 percent. Data for census tracts with predominantly for-profit housing reveal significant change in the demography of Loisaida between 1980 and 1990.[3]

Although the increase in total population of East Village residents was negligible, changes in its composition were striking (DeGiovanni 1988). There was significant change in the level of educational attainment of neighborhood residents. The percentage of East Villagers over twenty-five years of age with college degrees increased 14.5 percent, as compared to 8.4 percent for all of Manhattan. The percent change between 1980 and 1990 in the East Village median household income as indexed to Manhattan increased as well by 19 percent (U.S. Census of Population and Housing 1980 and 1990).

Restructuring and Displacement in the East Village

Changes in the means of displacing low-income tenants and attracting more affluent ones have changed dramatically throughout the 1980s and 1990s. Developers have shown exceptional tenacity in their efforts to subvert the East Village's working-class character. For many of the low-income residents who have endured years of abandonment and then gentrification, relationships with landlords have been a constant struggle to maintain residence. Such is the case of Carmello, a resident of Loisaida. Carmello's story is typical of many Lower East Side residents. He was born in Puerto Rico and arrived in Williamsburg, Brooklyn in 1951 as a young man along with his sister who had been recruited on the island to work at Brooklyn's American Razor Corporation. Soon after their arrival, he found a job unloading leather canvas in the South of Houston industrial area and he moved in with relatives on the Lower East Side to be closer to work. Eight and a half years later, Carmello was let go when the firm, like many others, closed down. Carmello began receiving welfare. Later, he applied for and was granted a Section 8 housing subsidy for an apartment on Avenue C. He lived there throughout the late 1960s and 1970s in a building where all the occupants were Puerto Rican, unemployed, on welfare, and living in Section 8 subsidized apartments. Carmello remembers when Loisaida Avenue (Avenue C) was lined with Hispanic specialty shops, restaurants, bakeries, and funeral homes. Carmello also remembers when residents and businesses left in the mid-1970s, terrified by fires that had decimated blocks of buildings. The sudden appearance of drug dealers coupled with a progressive feeling of isolation from the rest of the city made Loisaida inhospitable to long-term residents. Many fled the area for Williamsburg, East Harlem, and other neighborhoods within New York. In the 1980s, new construction, rehabilitation, and an increase in the number of non-Latino residents occurred. Throughout these years of abandonment and then gentrification Carmello remained in his East Village apartment—2A at 133 Avenue C. By 1988, half of his original neighbors had left, replaced by college students and artists who were entering the neighborhood in greater numbers. In 1988, Carmello succumbed to his landlord's ambitious efforts to remove remaining low-income tenants and renovate their apartments. After three consecutive winters of sporadic heat and two years on a waiting list for public housing, Carmello gladly took the

$5,000 offered by his landlord and moved to the Jacob Riis Public Houses on Avenue D.

The variety of displacement tactics experienced by Carmello and others of his cohort differed in their effectiveness, in their degree of direct and indirect coercion, and in their geographic scale. The periodic changes and innovations in displacement techniques did not occur arbitrarily but were determined strategically. The emergence of new displacement strategies reflected real estate capitalists' quest to bypass the legal- structural conditions of New York rental housing, to co-opt state investment incentive programs, to further the influx of new real estate investment capital and to circumvent organized and unorganized forms of resistance.

Legal-structural factors specific to the New York City housing market prevented the wholesale dislodging of incumbent residents and immediate redevelopment. First, no large-scale public-private development initiative or urban renewal plan existed that would allow developers and the state to undertake evictions and condemnation through eminent domain. Consequently, redevelopment was protracted and carried out initially by individual entrepreneurs and eventually medium-sized real estate firms (Mele 1994). Second, most low-income renters lived in apartments with state-regulated rental leases. These leases, which dictated the allowable percentage of rent increase charged at each renewal, gave legal tenure to low-income renters. As a class of renters, these regulations protected against unwarranted or wholesale evictions. For an individual renter, however, that protection was less certain when confronted with an array of displacement tactics.

At the same time that New York housing market regulations prevented the immediate and full-scale transformation of the East Village into a higher rent district, private development incentive programs offered by the state and local governments in the 1980s undermined the housing security of low-income tenants. Responding to widespread housing disinvestment and abandonment in the 1970s, state-subsidized programs were initiated to attract capital investment back into inner city housing. A variety of programs offered temporary tax abatements and exemptions on a case-by-case basis to encourage building owners to make capital improvements to units within their buildings. As individual landlords made renovations to their buildings, the potential rental value of the units (especially those occupied by low-income tenants with protected leases) escalated (Sites 1994). As a result, subsidized development intensified displacement pressures. As allowed by law, East Village landlords typically utilized these programs to renovate units that were emptied; units housing existing long-term, low-income residents were rarely modernized.

A third factor that shaped the contours of displacement was the escalation of the stakes in the local real estate game. Redevelopment was incremental and cumulative. As larger amounts of capital were invested in the East Village housing market, the typical landowner shifted from the individual to corporate real estate development firms and property management companies. These new actors triggered changes in tactics to rid the housing market of low-income renters and to attract more affluent tenants. As investment capital continued to flow into the physical redevelopment of the neighborhood, the level of compulsion of new displacement techniques diminished. The effect of involuntary outmigration of low-income tenants, however, continued unabated (DeGiovanni 1987).

What combined effect did rent regulations, state investment incentives, and the rising property values have upon the shape of new displacement tactics? In the initial stages of reinvestment, displacement was coercive. New owners, especially speculators, were anxious to rid buildings of low-income tenants. Emptied buildings commanded higher resale value. To circumvent state rental restrictions, illegal tactics were often utilized to empty buildings of low-income tenants. Withholding essential heat and hot water, renting adjacent units to drug users and torching emptied units to terrorize remaining tenants into relocating, dominated the first stages of development (DeGiovanni 1987; *New York Newsday* 1989). In one instance that would galvanize the antidevelopment sentiments of community organizations and local residents, displacement led to the death of a handicapped tenant, Lincoln Swados. Swados, an amputee confined to a wheelchair, lived alone in the storefront of an East 4th Street tenement. He was sued for eviction in 1988 by new owners of the building, GLM, a property development corporation based in Washington, D.C. Swados was to vacate the unit in February 1989 according to settlement terms and the building was to be renovated. Before Swados vacated his home, workers erected a construction shed enclosing the buildings' storefronts including Swado's unit. Although GLM representatives claim they left Swados a key to the shed, Swados was trapped in his apartment when he became ill. He was found dead three days later (Nachtgeist 1989).

According to housing organizers, Lincoln Swados' death was an extreme case of the everyday harassment and disregard for tenants' well-being. The use of illegal means was customary for emptying out entire buildings where an overwhelming proportion of the units were rent-regulated apartments with below-market rents. Many of the displaced residents, especially older Latinos, were less likely to register complaints of tenant abuse due to fear, language barriers, a lack of access to legal assistance, and shared stories of city housing agencies unresponsive to complaints.

As development ventures increased and the number of rehabilitated units swelled, larger segments of low-income renters were affected as well by exclusionary displacement (Marcuse 1985). Apartments vacated by low-income tenants were quickly renovated and leased at significantly higher rents, thus diminishing the supply of available low-income housing. As in other gentrifying neighborhoods in New York, low-income families were being priced out of the market for renovated apartments (DeGiovanni and Minnite 1991). Subsequently, overcrowding in low-income housing units increased (DeGiovanni 1987) and low-income residents were spatially concentrated in blocks peripheral to the core of redevelopment efforts. Many displaced Latino residents doubled up in the area's city-owned and managed housing. According to the 1990 census, Latinos constituted 79 percent of the residents of the public housing towers situated along Avenue D. In the adjacent census tracts, they constitute approximately 45 percent (U.S. Census of Population and Housing 1990). Many of these tenants depended on the city's below-market rents to maintain homes in the neighborhood. Consequently, city-owned housing was a buttress against development-driven displacement.

Organized neighborhood housing coalitions, such as the Metropolitan Council on Housing, Cooper Square, Good Ole Lower East Side (GOLES), Coalition Housing, Pueblo Nuevo, It's Time, MFY Legal Services and, especially, the umbrella organization to which many belonged, the Lower East Side Planning Council, ran increasingly effective campaigns against harassment and evictions. Rent strikes, the dissemination of tenant rights information and the monitoring of speculator activities slowed the pace of developers' land-grab and partially retained the area for some low- and moderate-income residents.

By the mid-1980s realtors' efforts to displace low-income residents in the East Village showed mixed and uneven results. As structural-legal factors and organized resistance prevented large-scale physical displacement, the removal of tenants occurred gradually unit by unit. Consequently, East Village rents and income, poverty, and education levels were intensely stratified, reflecting the arrival of new residents alongside a declining cohort of older ones. Most significantly, stratification was evident at the smallest geographic scale, the block level and, frequently, within individual apartment buildings (DeGiovanni 1987). Landlords clearly feared renovations would create incentives for long-term residents to remain. The wide discrepancies in living conditions that often existed between the poorest and the wealthiest residents housed in the same apartment building were striking. Within typical tenement buildings with twenty units, it was routine to find apartments in conditions untouched since the turn of the century adjacent to completely renovated and modernized units. Tenants included those who had leased apartments in the 1960s and those who had just arrived; dense multigenerational networks of Puerto Rican families; college students living with roommates; drug addicts, blue-collar workers, and single mothers, alongside fashion designers, musicians, and management trainees. Many of the unrenovated apartments were substandard one-bedroom floor-throughs (also referred to as railroad or shotgun apartments). Turn-of-the-century closeted commodes were common as were bathtubs in kitchens that simultaneously served as workspace by adding a hinged lid as a countertop. These units were homes to low-income Puerto Rican families who had settled there in the 1960s, weathered the decline in the 1970s, and resisted the displacement efforts of landlords in the 1980s. Since their rents were state regulated and they had remained in their original apartments for decades, many families paid rents less than $400 per month. Within the same buildings, other units reflected a different reality. Whereas low-income tenants lived in apartments that were uniformly substandard, the majority of their new neighbors lived in renovated and modernized apartments. New tenants were households consisting of two or more unrelated individuals who were younger, well-educated, non-Hispanic whites who shared rents ranging between $800 to $1,200 per month.

Despite the inequities between the living situations of the old and new tenants, there was little hostility between the two. Although new and old neighbors of the same building rarely interacted socially, there were adjustments to be made for both. For some of the remaining low-income, older Latino residents, the presence of new tenants meant that the harsher tactics—no heat, hot water, or repairs—would diminish. New tenants, on the other hand, were often surprised by the circumstances of living in a transitional building especially given the high rents paid, as the experience of one new resident of a walkup on 10th Street and Avenue C demonstrates:

> We moved into the apartment in November, when the weather wasn't so cold. Typically, the radiators turned cold early Saturday mornings, when no one was in the management office, and heat would not be restored until Monday afternoons. When I or my roommates complained to the management company, they'd act concerned and promised to "get right on it." We were always told the oil had run out or a new part for the heater was on order. I asked our neighbor, a Puerto Rican woman I befriended, if this was routine. She seemed surprised by my question and, apparently, by my naivete. She said she rarely called the landlord. They told her some time ago that the heater was old and, given the cold outdoor temperatures, it couldn't keep up. The landlord couldn't afford to replace the heater anytime soon, so there was no use in complaining. Our persistent calls occasionally brought us more heat. After that, whenever it was cold she'd ask us to call the landlord for her.[4]

As the demography of the tenements tilted in favor of the newcomers, the more coercive displacement tactics slowly gave way to benign ones. In buildings where low-income tenants remained the majority, the provision of services was spotty and unreliable. In buildings where units were occupied by both newcomers and incumbent residents, reconstruction was nearly constant, as landlords renovated individual units one at a time as they were vacated by poor, Latino tenants. The withholding of maintenance or heat affected all apartments in a building, including newly occupied and renovated units. Landlords instead resorted to buying out tenants —offering sums at times in excess of $10,000 to vacate. Buy-outs were attractive to many low-income residents.

Resistance to Displacement: East Village Style

A return visit to the Christodora House two years and one month after its grand reopening finds the neighborhood in the midst of social transformation and increasingly uneasy about it. Around 3:00 A.M on August 8, 1988, Father George Kuhn, a parish priest from St. Brigid's Catholic Church one block south of the Christodora, stood between a cordon of police in full riot gear and about 200 jeering protestors in an attempt to defuse the tense standoff over control of the intersection of

8th Street and Avenue A. Earlier that evening, shortly after 12:00 A.M., riot police squared off with a group of organized demonstrators protesting the newly enforced midnight curfew in Tompkins Square Park, a well- attended 24–hour neighborhood meeting place.[5] Between midnight and 3:00 A.M., the police widened the scope of conflict in what amounted to a full-scale invasion of the East Village. Backed by helicopters, advanced communication vehicles, and the tacit permission of police commanders, many officers, their badges removed to avoid identification, meted "street justice" indiscriminately. It was vengeance for months (if not years) of taunting by local antigentrifiers who equated police presence with landlord interests. Forty-four people, many of whom were bystanders caught in the fray, were injured in what is now known as the Tompkins Square Police Riot (Hassan 1988).[6]

The priest was finally able to calm tensions long enough for the crowd of demonstrators to "elect" two or three spokespersons to negotiate a truce. Before setting a time and place—one week later at the Ninth Precinct station house—for a community meeting to address the evening's mayhem, members of the makeshift delegation voiced some of the issues angering the demonstrators. "There's been no dialogue. Rents are going up."[7] It soon became obvious that the park's curfew enforcement was the flash point of deeper tensions over control of the redevelopment of the neighborhood.

Before dawn, a handful of protestors, feeling victorious from the police back-down, descended upon the touchstone of real estate colonization, the Christodora House. Using parts from a police wooden saw-horse barricade, they rammed the glass doors of the entrance way, ripping down a light fixture and overturning a potted fern. All the while they chanted "Die Yuppie Scum!" Outside, to the cheers of a small band of onlookers, they mounted a banner carried earlier in the evening; it read, "Gentrification + Class War = Genocide." Clearly, if gentrification was to change the (ill-defined) character of the East Village, locals were not going to take it so easily.

Indiscriminate displacement tactics were also being challenged on a daily basis. Popular resistance to the sweeping away of the East Village's working-class image emerged as a culture of protest against the bland, middle-class aesthetics of gentrification. The "Die Yuppie Scum" message was sprawled on buildings and sidewalks throughout the neighborhood. "Mug a Yuppie" and other neighborhood graffiti blatantly urged locals to harass newcomers and to boycott upscale boutiques and groceries. Locally based newspapers, such as the *East Villager* and the *Lower East Side News*, railed against realtors and their plans to homogenize the diverse character of the East Village. Demonstrations and clashes between activists and police continued between 1988 and 1990 over Tompkins Square Park, squatter rebellions and homeless evictions. The coverage of these events did not play well into developers' ambitions of upgrading the East Village rental market. Despite the best intentions of preserving the working-class character of the East Village, many participants of demonstrations and daily resistance included few of the low-income residents threatened by displacement; most were young, white, college-educated newcomers who, as recent renters, contributed (albeit unwilling) to the processes of displacement and gentrification.

Other ironies emerged in the unfolding of the struggle between developers and residents. In the midst of intensive neighborhood redevelopment, pockets of the East Village remained notorious as "protected" and nonviolent locations for drug distribution, especially the dealing of heroin and cocaine. Dense and complex social networks of low-income residents coupled their state rent-regulated status and participation in the informal economy of drug sales to construct elaborate "safe zones" that presented an effective yet unorganized (and unanticipated) resistance to the emptying out of buildings and entire blocks of residents.[8] Many of these city block-long dealing operations were Latino-owned, were decades old, and employed residents in a complex division of labor modeled after the Puerto Rican neighborhood *padrone* (provider) system. Local participation in the trade was extensive and boundaries between licit (e.g., a grocery store worker) and illicit (drug dealer) occupations were permeable. Family members and neighbors acted as rooftop whistlers and lookouts for potential police sweeps, as client chaperons, and directly as dealers.

In contrast to that of adjacent blocks that succumbed first to abandonment and later to gentrification, the community life of these blocks was remarkably stable. Residential displacement and turnover were minimal: most tenants had lived on the block since birth or had arrived from Puerto Rico in the early 1960s. The drug trade and its somewhat impermeable social network had unintentionally acted as a barrier to displacement pressures. In a few instances, partial revenues from drug dealing had been funnelled into building maintenance and upkeep. On this same block, the principal dealer who had taken seriously his role as neighborhood father-figure and provider sponsored a summer softball league and offered free Tae-Kwan-Do lessons to neighborhood children. Community organizations disavowed the neighborhood drug markets and were critical of the city's lack of law enforcement in certain known drug locations. At the same time they were critical of campaigns such as Operation Pressure Point and other drug enforcement campaigns that largely targeted areas where gentrification was well under way.

Contributing further irony, these same blocks had begun to see a gradual increase in newcomers drawn to the cheap rents of the few available unrenovated apartments and to an added "safety" factor. Since all activities on the block were monitored by residents involved in the drug trade, a remarkable social order was maintained on this block; outdoor drug consumption, petty crimes, apartment break-ins, and assaults were atypical. One tenant of the only renovated building on a drug dealer-controlled block spoke of her housing experience in the fall of 1989:

> I'll never forget the first night in my new apartment. I'd thought it would be my last. When the rental agent showed me the apartment in the middle of the afternoon, the place seemed liveable and the building was clean. Although the block was farther east than I wanted, it looked harmless. I had heard horror stories about living this close to the river but I also heard it was getting better. Kids playing, people shopping, nothing unusual. That night things changed. A few doors from my home a Latino guy in his early twenties stopped me, asked me my name and asked me what I needed and where I was going. When I pointed to my building he asked which apartment was mine. He seemed to believe me only when I produced a set of house keys. As I approached my front door another young guy exited the building and began the same inquisition. Before I could say anything, my first encounter (his name is Ric) motioned to let me in. I didn't know what to think. That was five months ago. Ric deals but I think of him as the building's doorman and as a friend. He looks out for me. He knows my friends and ushers them in or takes messages from them when I'm not home. He'll sign for package deliveries if you ask him. He's lent me money when I'm short on cash. All of the drug dealers and old-timers know me and my schedule. There's more of sense of community here than uptown.[9]

This "order" was imposed and maintained by dealers to prevent unwanted police intrusions that would interrupt drug sales transactions. Operating as classic free-riders, new residents welcomed unquestioningly the added personal security found on these blocks. In most cases, dealer networks and new residents developed a "live-and-let-live" attitude toward each other.

For real estate developers and landlords, resistance to physical displacement and persistence of pockets of low-income residents reinforced the notion that, despite inroads, the East Village was only partially gentrified and was not likely to succumb to a full-scale gentrification of the type occurring in other Manhattan neighborhoods or in neighborhoods of cities such as Washington, D.C. and Philadelphia. By 1989, gentrification appeared stalled for several reasons. First, a stalemate existed between developers and community activists, who had effectively halted the physical displacement of low-income tenants as a continuing strategy for redevelopment. In addition, the typical gentrifiers— white middle-class professionals—did not show as much interest in settling in the neighborhood as realtors had anticipated. Finally, the luxury end of New York's residential housing market bottomed out, leaving available scores of existing units.[10] Redevelopment of the East Village appeared no longer lucrative.

Or so it seemed. Although the strategy of upper-middle class revitalization was thwarted, real estate developers and landlords in the 1990s have capitalized on the unique features of the East Village's social and cultural landscape, thereby transforming many of the former constraints to displacement and redevelopment into new opportunities.

Reinventing the East Village

Real estate developers and landlords have recently turned to a less coercive and indirect form of displacement. Rather than attempt to impose upon the neighborhood a likeness of a sanitized, middle-class "village," developers have sought to play up the sociocultural image of the East Village for consumption by nontraditional gentrifier households composed of multiple, younger, and unrelated individuals with independent incomes. Real estate actors have reversed their strategy of completely erasing the "downtown" image of the East Village. They have instead appropriated the neighborhood's historical reputation for cultural diversity and its recent status as an incubator of prospective cultural trends and have packaged them as amenities for lucrative niche residential markets. Although remaining low-income and minority residents were not directly threatened with removal from their homes, this strategy has caused exclusionary or "slow-burner" displacement.

The link between the East Village and cultural forms is not new. Historically, the cultural, ethnic, and racial diversity of the East Village has influenced the creation of innovative and experimental forms of art, music, and writing that countered dominant mainsteam forms of culture. Several genres that have surfaced since the 1950s either were launched in the East Village or were made popular there. Abstract Expressionist painters in the 1950s were centered in studios and makeshift gallery spaces on East 10th Street where Willem De Kooning and Jasper Johns held early shows. Beat Generation writers Allen Ginsburg, Jack Kerouac, and William Burroughs lived intermittently in the East Village and produced and performed their work there. In the emerging enclave of Loisaida, Puerto Rican writers thrived in their new urban landscape and established the Nuyorican Poets Cafe. In the 1960s, the East Village emerged as the east coast counterpart to San Francisco's Haight Ashbury. The music, art, and style of hippie culture was situated on the east-west transverse of the East Village: Saint Mark's Place from Astor Place to Tompkins Square Park, with the corner of Second Avenue and Saint Mark's the center point. "A massive influx of boutiques, antique fur stores, hairdressing shops, and pizza and ice cream beaneries," reported the *Village Voice* (1971), "turned the block [St. Marks's] into a limp Times Square." As thousands were drawn to an East Village transformed by the philosophy of nonconformity and self-expression, the area gained a reputation as a mecca for practitioners and observers of a variety of counter- or alternative cultures. The era was brief, however, as the uniqueness of hippie culture languished after having been commercialized, mainstreamed, and dispersed to communities in other cities and the suburbs. One by one, the landmarks of counterculture disappeared from the landscape; in 1971, two music/night spots—Andy Warhol's Electric Circus and the Fillmore East—were closed.

The eventual demise of East Village hippie culture foreshadowed a trend that has beset most if not all countercultural movements that have since been associated with the neighborhood. In the past fifteen years, the commercialization of the East Village culture incubator has been accelerated. Art galleries promoting the local art scene materialized in the 1980s and contributed to the commodification of downtown culture (Deutsche and Ryan 1984). Key downtown artists, such as Jean-Michel Basquiat and pop artists Keith Haring and Kenny Scharf, were key figures whose eventual fame mythologized the East Village's reputation as a countercultural enclave. Basquiat began his career spray-painting social and political messages on building walls in lower Manhattan, signing his work SAMO (copyright symbol) ("same old shit"). By the late 1970s, Basquiat hooked up with a loose network of like-minded artists and musicians centered in East Village bars and night-clubs and began to exhibit in "underground" art shows, where his work was "discovered" by the established art world. Other art and entertainment forms have since been invented or played out in the East Village. The Pyramid Club on Avenue A showcased East Village drag-transvestitism and gave an early venue to RuPaul, the six- foot-plus African-American drag singer/performer who single-handedly glamorized and mainstreamed drag culture on American television and radio. The roots of Karen Finley's performance art, which rankled the nerves of critics of the National Endowment for the Arts (from whom she received a grant) during the Bush presidency, may be traced to the alternative clubs and performance spaces found in the East Village.

The success of the culture industry in the East Village is due in part to the globalization of U.S. entertainment and culture and, simultaneously, to the corporate promotion of cultural forms geared toward specialized or "niche" consumer markets. In essence, these developments in the entertainment and culture industries thrive on a space like the East Village where new and potentially successful (profitable) ideas are spawned.[11]

The real estate industry has been quick to capitalize on the implications for the housing market. Throughout the many cultural transformations of the 1950s, 1960s, and 1970s, it was the writers, musicians, artists, and others who sought to carve out an enclave for experimentation and autonomy. Beginning in the 1980s, however, the connection between the East Village and alternative cultural forms included other actors who saw an opportunity for development — the city and real estate developers. In 1982, Mayor Koch's administration developed the Artists Homeownership Program (AHOP) to convert city-owned properties into artists' housing. AHOP was a blatant attempt to recreate SoHo-styled gentrification in devalorized neighborhoods—that is, creating a domino effect of redevelopment by harnessing the investment allure of the increasingly commodified art world. The program was never enacted, however, as it met strong community opposition; it was defeated in the city's Board of Estimate in 1983 (Sites 1994).

Real estate developers have been more successful in spatializing the cultural image of the East Village, embracing its most profitable elements and discarding others. A prime example of attaching cultural notoriety with bricks and mortar is Baby Jane Holzer's ventures in East Village real estate. Holzer was a socialite well-connected to Andy Warhol films and has since kept alive memories of Warhol's Factory in her capacity as a real estate developer. Holzer personalized her buildings by giving them names and renovating them according to designs that reflect her interpretation of the East Village, including oak floors and exposed bricks (Samuels 1990). For other lesser-known developers the nexus of culture and neighborhood had become increasingly profitable. As one local rental agent put it:

> It used to be that renters lived in the East Village as a last resort because the rents were cheap, as were the restaurants and green grocers. Today, our tenants do not want to live in nicer neighborhoods, like the Upper East Side or even the West Village for that matter. In fact, when you take into account the [smaller] size of East Village apartments, the rents are roughly comparable. Those neighborhoods sell quiet streets, quaint stores and safe buildings. Down here, we're selling action. They're looking for where the action is and they know its in the East Village.[12]

The East Village has been packaged as a very chaotic version of a South Street Seaport or Baltimore's Inner Harbor. What has been consumed here by suburban teens on weekends or by corporate arts and entertainment professionals is an image of danger, seediness, and the mystique of "living on the edge." The area's rawness has been cleverly (and perversely) packaged as the suspense, intrigue, and adventure of a "lawless frontier" (Smith 1992) for consumption by young, white, middle-class tenants who desire to live out, if only for a few years, their dystopian fantasies. The contradiction is troubling, but has been seemingly profitable for developers. "The neighborhood's funkiness," reads a description in *The New York Times* real estate (1992) supplement, "seems to include graffiti-covered buildings, garbage strewn by the homeless collecting redeemables and heavy drug traffic. The allure of bohemian decadence keeps housing prices up."

East Village writer Joshua Whalen's short story, "Venus," tells the story of the meeting of a young man, the narrator, and a woman, Caroline, in a setting of urban change. Caroline moved to the East Village from Wyoming where she "dreamed and schemed of going anywhere, anywhere else at all, but especially here, the place she'd read about in novels and seen in movies and heard about in songs." Their relationship became ensconced in the East Village "scene." When Caroline was not working at a local illegal after-hours nightclub, the two spent their time together in local bars, coffeeshops, and Ukranian diners. All was shattered when the city and its police department conducted one of their periodic crackdowns on East Village vice.

> Suddenly, the easiness and comfortable decay that had been the hallmarks of the Lower East Side began to change. . . . Every street from Delancey to 14th was flooded with cops of every description. Systematically, a block, sometimes only a building at a time, they swept through the slum, securing territory, ostensibly to wipe out the drug traffic that had prospered for almost two decades in the battered tenements, abandoned, fire-gutted shells, and garbage-strewn lots. However that may have been, whatever their alleged intent, in their wake fell every after-hours club, every seedy bar, every street peddler, every graffiti artist. . . . If I was stung [by the events], however, Caroline, who had only arrived a year earlier, was shattered. . . . Now and then we'd try to talk, but things had changed. There wasn't a beautiful magical village of random factors outside our door anymore. There was only Prague, or Chile (Whalen 1990, 96–97).

No matter that the crackdown was short-lived, this passage illustrates the romanticization of a part of the East Village that many lifelong, low-income residents have fought to eliminate. In a disturbing way, the remaining community of low-income and disadvantaged residents and homeless persons served as a backdrop to the latest manifestation of development. The poverty and urban decay that developers had once tried to eliminate by physically displacing the poorest tenants but in large measure had failed were increasingly put to the employ of profit making. Here displacement was not physical but social as a community of more affluent newcomers had been superimposed upon the remaining working-class, low-income one. The social problems of drugs, unemployment, and privation continued to plague the residents of many blocks in the East Village residents but were now serving as allure. An advertisement in the May 31, 1994 edition of the *Village Voice* for an apartment rental in a nongentrified block of the East Village issued an exclusive dare for the adventurous apartment hunter.

> 4th Street East—Very Far East. Believe it or not renovated 4 room apartment $800. Not for everybody but perfect for some.

Conclusion

Within a span of ten years, displacement tactics in the East Village have ranged from the physical dislocation of low-income tenants to the exclusionary displacement associated with the appropriation of the neighborhood's "bohemian" reputation and its role in the growing culture and entertainment industries. The factors that have triggered this shift include state urban development policies, increasing levels of capital investment in rental housing and community resistance. The tenacity of developers in inventing new ways of displacing low-income tenants and transforming land use is striking. Their cunning, however, is matched only by the innovative forms of resistance constructed by the community. From this particular case, we learn that the trajectory of residential displacement and neighborhood change is not unswerving but one that is fraught with variation, unevenness and unpredictability.

Those same characteristics apply to the struggle over displacement and development in the East Village today. Whereas developers have sought to continue to displace the low-income community through packaging it for a specific market of housing consumers, neighborhood housing coalitions have successfully set aside units safeguarded from displacement. Since 1992, several blocks along Avenue C have been reconstructed under a 50/50 Cross Subsidy Plan that had been negotiated by the city and the local community board (Abu-Lughod 1994a). Both real estate and local housing coalitions share in the disposition of these city-owned lots and buildings. The plan proposed to allocate 1000 dwelling units in existing city-owned tenements for low-to-middle-income occupants, to be rehabilitated using revenue gained from the sale of a comparable number of empty lots to real estate developers constructing market-value units. By temporarily (and, in some cases, permanently) securing the disposition of these properties as low-income housing units, the potential for private development to engulf the area has once again been thwarted.[13] Housing organizations, it would appear, have learned to depend less on government protection (in the form of rent regulations, code enforcement, etc.) of low-income neighborhoods. Mutual housing associations have struck a hard blow to displacement by preventing certain properties from being returned to the private market. The precedent is important. Community ownership and disposition of housing units have turned the logic of urban accumulation on its head by decommodifying urban space. Without neighborhood space being produced and reproduced by developers as a commodity, the uncertain living situations of many low-income residents have been potentially improved.

Notes

1. I conducted participant-observation and interviews with residents, community organizers and real estate actors in the East Village between 1988 and 1992 and again in 1994 for a larger project. See Mele (1993).
2. Quote from interview on realtors' role in 1980s development with a real estate executive of property management company operating in the East Village.
3. Data related to demographic changes in Loisaida are from 1980 and 1990 census figures for census tracts 22.02, 26.01, 26.02, 28, 30.02, 32, and 34.
4. Interview, February 15, 1988.
5. Tompkins Square Park was known as the neighborhood's "lung"—the only accessible open space in the midst of the dense settlement of airless tenements. The summer of 1988 was particularly hot and humid and the park was utilized day and night. Resident complaints over late-night noise prompted the Avenue A Block Association to petition the local Community Board on June 28, 1988 to pass a resolution to enforce the curfew. In the aftermath of the riot, the resolution in support of curfew enforcement was equated with support for gentrification. Finger-pointing and denials over responsibility for the resolution further divided community leaders over the gentrification issue.
6. In one well-publicized incident of police violence, "an officer [was] seen jamming his nightstick into the spokes of a passing bicycle. The rider fell to the ground and was set upon and clubbed by several officers" (*The New York Times*, 1988).
7. Videotape of riot by Clayton Patterson, August 7–8, 1993 (field notes of video by Janet Abu-Lughod). A fuller treatment of the Tompkins Square Riot and its aftermath can be found in Abu- Lughod 1994b.
8. Evidence for the following analysis is derived from field work conducted between 1988 and 1991 in two blocks with extensive drug-dealing activity. See also the recent newspaper article on drugs and police corruption in the New York Police Department's East Village precinct by James Rutenberg (1994).
9. Interview, March 3, 1990.
10. Luxury and upper-middle class housing units were adversely affected by the decline in the real estate market. The middle-income rental market, however, remained stable and has recently shown growth. According to rental agents interviewed in May 1994, rents in neighborhoods that were extensively developed in the 1980, such as Chelsea, Hell's Kitchen, and the East Village, have steadily climbed since 1991.
11. For an overview of the media successes of the commercialization of downtown Manhattan in the past decade, see the June 1994 edition of *Paper* magazine.
12. From interview, May 27, 1994 with rental agent and partner in a property management companies dealing with East Village properties.
13. Community land trusts and public-private housing coalitions operate differently and have distinct forms of ownership. Local not-for-profit housing associations retain indefinite ownership of land in community land trusts. Associations sell the

housing units to individual low-income residents and lend money to occupants for renovations. Occupants are permitted to sell their property only at original cost in addition to improvements made. Private-public coalitions create an equity trust from corporate investments. Using trust money, coalitions purchase and rehabilitate properties. These units are rented as low-income housing for a period of ten to fifteen years. They may be sold to private developers at market-rate only after the period expires. Both of these community redevelopment initiatives attempt to direct growth to include the needs of at-risk populations, thus curtailing displacement. See Abu-Lughod 1994a.

References

Abu-Lughod, Janet et al. (1994). *From Urban Village to East Village: The Battle for New York's Lower East Side.* Oxford: Basil Blackwell.

Abu-Lughod, Janet (1994a). "Defending the Cross-Subsidy Plan: The Tortoise Wins Again." In Abu-Lughod et al.

Abu-Lughod, Janet (1994b). "The Battle for Tompkins Square Park." In Abu-Lughod et al.

Barrett, A. Lee and David C. Hodge (1984). "Social Differentials in Metropolitan Residential Displacement." In J. John Palen and Bruce London, eds., *Gentrification, Displacement and Neighborhood Revitalization.* Albany: State University of New York Press, 1984, pp. 141–42.

Cincin-Sain, B. (1980). "The Costs and Benefits of Neighborhood Revitalization." In *Urban Revitalization,* D.B. Rosenthal, ed. Urban Affairs Annual Reviews, vol. 18. Beverly Hills, CA: Sage Publications, pp. 49-75.

DeGiovanni, Frank (1987). *Displacement Pressures on the Lower East Side.* New York: The Community Service Society.

DeGiovanni, Frank and Lorraine Minnite (1991). "Patterns of Neighborhood Change." In John Hull Mollenkopf and Manuel Castells, eds. *Dual City: Restructuring New York.* New York: Russell Sage Foundation.

Feagin, Joe R. and Robert Parker (1990). *Building American Cities: The Urban Real Estate Game.* Englewood Cliffs, NJ: Prentice Hall.

Gordon, Diana (1994). "An Identity of Impermanence: A Resident's View of Conflict on Tompkins Square Park." In Abu-Lughod, et al.

Gottdiener, Mark (1985). *The Social Production of Urban Space.* Austin: The University of Texas Press.

Hartman, Chester (1979a). "Comment on H. J. Sumka's 'Neighborhood Revitalization and Displacement: A Review of the Evidence.'" *Journal of the American Planning Association,* vol. 45, pp. 488–90.

Hartman, Chester (1979b). "Displacement: A Not So New Problem." *Social Policy,* vol. 9, No. 5, pp. 22–27.

Hassan, Jennifer (1988). "On the Road to Chaos." *East Villager,* vol. 22, no. 9, September 1988.

Marcuse, Peter (1985). "Gentrification, Abandonment, and Displacement: Connections, Causes, and Policy Responses in New York City." *Journal of Urban and Contemporary Law,* vol. 28, pp. 195– 240.

Mele, Christopher (1993). "Reinventing the East Village of New York: Capitalist Investment Strategies from 1860 to 1990." PhD dissertation, New School for Social Research.

Mele, Christopher (1994). "The Process of Gentrification in Alphabet City." In Abu-Lughod, et al.

Nachtgeist, Laurence (1989). "A Kinder, Gentler Gentrification." *East Villager*, vol. 23, no.4.

New York Newsday (1989). "Not-So-Gentle Gentrification," by Sylvia Moreno, January 23, p. 7.

Real Estate Newsletter (1985). "Lower East Side Real Estate Profile: Speculators Less Active, Renovators Push to Get Market Rate Projects Going, City Mulls Sale of In-Rem Buildings, Yuppies Like it Even if Drug Dealers Share the Streetscape," vol. 16, no. 51, November 4.

Rutenberg, James (1994). "Why the Ninth Precinct Has Such a Bad Rap." *The Manhattan Spirit*, vol. 10, no. 21, June 1, 1994, p. 12.

Samuels, David (1990). "She Put the 'Trific' in Gentrification." *Interview*, February, p. 52.

Sassen, Saskia (1991). *The Global City: New York, London, Tokyo*. Princeton, NJ: Princeton University Press, pp. 256–64.

Sites, William (1994). "Public Action: New York City Policy and the Gentrification of the Lower East Side." In Abu-Lughod et al.

Smith, Michael Peter (1988). *City, State and Market: The Political Economy of Urban Society*. New York: Basil Blackwell.

Smith, Neil (1992). "New City, New Frontier: The Lower East Side as Wild, Wild West." In Michael Sorkin, ed., *Variations on A Theme Park*. New York: Noonday Press, pp. 61–93.

Sumka, H. J. (1979). "Neighborhood Revitalization and Displacement: A Review of the Evidence." *Journal of the American Planning Association*, vol.45, pp. 480-87.

The New York Times (1988). "Heavily Tested by the Crowd in Tompkins Square, Police Discipline Broke," August 14.

The New York Times (1992). "If You're Thinking of Living in the East Village," June 14, RE p. 7.

U.S. Department of Housing and Urban Development (1979). *Displacement Report*. Office of Policy Development and Research, Washington, D.C.: U.S. Department of Housing and Urban Development.

U.S. Department of Housing and Urban Development (1981). *Residential Displacement: An Update*. Office of Policy Development and Research, Washington, D.C.: U.S. Department of Housing and Urban Development.

Village Voice (1971). "One-Way Street," no date [from the City of New York Municipal Archives clipping file].

Weiler, Conrad (1978). "Reinvestment Displacement: HUD's Role in a New Housing Issue." Report prepared for the Office of Community Planning and Development, Washington, D.C.: U.S. Department of Housing and Urban Development.

Whalen, Joshua (1990). *"Venus" A Day in the Life: Tales from the Lower East*. New York: Evil Eye Books.

4

Resisting Racially Gendered Space: The Women of the St.Thomas Resident Council, New Orleans

Alma H. Young and Jyaphia Christos-Rodgers

In this study we examine the work that women of color who live in public housing are doing in their community to resist the impacts of urban restructuring on their lives. We view the St.Thomas Resident Council as an alternative institution that is engaged in a discourse of resistance. We contrast two cultures in their approaches to economic development: the dominant institutional culture and a culture of resistance. We aim to illustrate the consequences of the dominant institutional culture's development practices for this community of low-income African-American women and their families. We then show the women responding to these practices by calling local institutions to accountability.

First, we deconstruct the strategies for economic development which unreflectively assume privilege and drain low-income communities of resources. We show how race, class, and gender organize access to resources in the corporate city. These "privatized" cities are planned to make money serving privileged people and enormous amounts of resources, both private and public, are invested in them. These strategies emerge from the dominant discourses of urban development theory and practice.

Second, we examine an approach to community-based economic development taken by one community that resists the politics of difference in the urban environment. This community is composed of low-income African-American women and their families in New Orleans. Their resistance is embedded in an understanding that institutional relations shape the everyday world; they seek to invert those institutional relations and thus redefine the power relationship between those who live in low-income communities and those who work within the institutional context. In their strategies of resistance they have adopted a holistic approach to community, with an emphasis on institutional accountability, self-determination, and partnership.

Method of Inquiry

We begin our study from the observation that contemporary feminist social scientific inquiry has moved beyond a "sex roles" approach, to viewing gender as an active process that can be observed at the institutional level (Acker 1990). Similarly, an antiracist inquiry moves beyond a simple concern with overt acts of racial discrimination to a concern with race as an active process embedded within social institutions. This approach shifts the focus from the notion of gender and race as demographic variables to an understanding that "difference" organizes institutions that are linked to everyday life. We conceive of these linkages as culture and assume that inquiry must focus upon culture to understand the potential for social change embodied by resistance.

The importance of a multicultural analysis of "racially gendered institutions" (Anzaldua 1990) stems from the fact that such an approach does not regard social organization as static or "determined" but as actively structured by relations of privilege and oppression. These relations are expressed through processes of gender, race, and class. The urban environment is not a monolithic culture but is composed of many interacting cultural threads shaped by race, gender, and class, or "difference." Culture is historically situated and emerging, reflecting the shifts between agency and power (see Ong 1987). Thus culture does not merely act upon people; people actively participate in these relations. People who are oppressed may internalize that oppression or they may resist it. Here we present a culture of resistance to the dominant institutional culture within the context of urban economic restructuring. The way we get at culture is to analyze discourse.

What Smith (1987) has called the ruling relations and Foucault (1980) has called Power/Knowledge is empirically observable through "discourse." Discourse is a form of power that circulates within the social field and can be likened to a conversation mediated by texts and practices (Smith 1987). This form of power can attach itself to strategies of domination and its acceptance (sometimes called internalized oppression) and to those of resistance.

By suggesting that the operations of modern power are in fact productive rather than repressive, Foucault argues that schemes of discursive practices are involved in the complex production of rituals, objects, and "truth." The effects of power/knowledge relations are to implant disciplinary techniques in bodies and human conduct, thereby complementing more overt forms of control in everyday life. Subtle, invisible forms of control are embodied in what we know as the dominant culture and found in the discourses of institutions.

Thus, when we analyze institutional discourses we illuminate the concerted activities of people at work producing, reproducing and resisting power or relations of ruling (Smith 1987). In this study, we look at a community of resistance whose work is building alternative institutions. This allows us to illuminate the incremental processes of social change brought about by a community of resistance in the context of urban restructuring.

Economic Development in the Dominant Culture

The crisis of the hypermobility of capital has led to economic and urban restructuring within the capitalist system. Part of that restructuring involves shifts in the geographical location of production, consumption, and residence that have profound implications for cities. City economies reflect the global change from a goods-producing to a service-producing economy. To regain profitability, the new regime of flexible accumulation stresses less specialized and more flexible labor. Mass consumption gives way to more differentiated consumption. The new regime also brings into being a new mode of regulation, that depresses both private wages and the social wage. The welfare state is dismantled in favor of a more entrepreneurial state (see Logan and Swanstrom 1990, 9–12).

One of the results is the corporate city, with its emphasis on growth and real estate development, especially in the central business district. The service-based corporate cities of late capitalism "shatter the notion of the city as public, as a delimited sphere in which persons are accountable and connected to one another. The city evolves into a chaotic form with a number of different layers" (Kling 1993, 37). In the corporate city, the professional services essential to technologically advanced economies become the predominant layer and are viewed as the primary sources of employment and wealth. Huge financial, banking, and corporate centers come to characterize the downtown built environment. In a further effort to make up for the loss of revenue and jobs associated with the decline in manufacturing employment, cities emphasize tourism and build convention centers, sports arenas, and upscale shopping malls. These attractions (e.g., Baltimore's Harbor Place, New York's South Street Seaport) are presented as urban spectacle (see Crawford 1992).

Government services, concerned with the maintenance and reproduction of the city, constitute another layer of employment. This government or "gatekeeping" layer has particular significance for this analysis for two reasons. First, these gatekeeping jobs tend to be raced and gendered and are largely filled by professional women. Second, these gatekeepers who implement programs serving low-income communities have a direct, immediate, and political impact on the lives of the people they serve. At another level is the "informal" economy—day laborers, workers in sweat shops, street vendors, and modest artisans. Much of this work is done by women, especially women of color, and children.

Corporate restructuring also leads to class recomposition—the transformation of wage and work relations to facilitate profitability. The class recomposition has led to greater social polarization, as the growth of high-wage jobs is accompanied by rapid expansion of low-wage jobs and the so-called informal sector, in which work remains undocumented and unprotected (Sassen 1988). As a result, individual wage inequality and family-income inequality are on the rise. Wage-inequality has increased dramatically because wage growth has slowed or reversed for many segments of the population, particularly those who are young, without college education, and/or African Americans and Hispanics.

Margrit Mayer (1991, 109) has described this as the "dual city," which is "determined by two equally dynamic sectors: the advanced services and high-tech sector and its unregulated, labor-intensive sector." This division of labor is reinforced by residential separation, with both residential and economic patterns responding to a legacy of racial separation in the United States. These divisions become all the more stark as the corporate city tends to neglect or dismantle public spaces and public sensibilities.

Instead of public spaces, urban areas become more differentiated as cities break down into "playgrounds for the affluent and wastelands for the low-paid service workers" (Dumm 1993, 192). Mobility from one area to the next is discouraged; in fact, in protected zones action is taken to retard possible invasions. Fear and hatred of others is encouraged by providing rationales for hierarchizing differences (Dumm 1993).

For those who can afford them, there is the development of communities of consumption. These residential communities privatize what would once have been considered public spaces by creating gates of entry and departure to provide security for those who live inside them. And in these communities anybody out of the ordinary sticks out, and people are quick to report anything or anybody suspicious. "Those who are different are perceived as dangerous. Those who are different are far away, spatially. Those who invade will be contained and removed" (Dumm 1993, 188). Other privatized areas include large retail/office/residential developments situated away from central cities. They are complemented by the frequently enclosed downtown malls, which offer a world within its enclosure.

The focus in all of these privatized spaces is upon a safe and sterile enclave in which the unpleasantries of inner-city decay are not visible to the residents, consumers, or office workers who fill them (see Crawford 1992). This focus has specific consequences for women of privilege, low-income women, and people of color. For example, while commercial interests work to provide a "safe" atmosphere conducive to middle-class women's spending time and money in them, working-class and low-income women tend to be the ones working the lower-end service sector jobs that keep the places running. At the same time, these low-income women often live in communities that have been left to decay, while public resources are put into these glitzy private enclaves. Even more, the issue of safety is fraught with racist overtones, as crime problems in the black community are used to justify the need for creating protected enclaves for those who can afford them. Thus safety, too, becomes a commodity to be purchased.

For the majority of poor people of color, the restructuring of the U.S. economy has been at their expense. The dismantling of the welfare system has had as its primary victims women and children (see Amott 1990). Taking up the slack in low-income black communities has been the move towards privatized social services such as religious charities. These services are provided without even the semblance of democratic accountability to which government agencies must adhere.

Beyond that, the state has engaged in systematic aggression towards poor people and people of color. For instance, from 1980 to 1990, the prison and jail population of the United States exploded (from 350,000 to 1,200,000). As of 1990, 23 percent of black men between the ages of eighteen and thirty in the United States were in prison, in jail, or on probation, compared to six percent of white men in the same age category (Dumm 1993, 190). With many poor men of color in prison, inner-city communities are left to be headed by women. These women find themselves in racially gendered spaces as a result of policies, both direct and default, that effect their ability to create resources that would be beneficial to themselves and their families (Spain 1993). Thus, economic development within the dominant culture works to the disadvantage of low-income women of color.

However, despite increasing economic and political domination, low-income women find ways to resist through organizations that allow them to discuss openly their situation, define themselves in terms different from those set by the authorities, and name their own strategies. In independently derived language and discourses there is the ability to demystify power and legitimize resistance against a corporate-controlled global economy.

Women's Community Based Development

In the above section we saw that localities have worked to entice private investment in order to strengthen downtowns and to generate new development. We also saw that the needs of low-income people tend to fall by the wayside as developers and local officials together work to build glitzy enclaves that draw affluent consumers. However, community-based development organizations work to address the needs of low-income families. Some of these groups work from the premise that economic issues cannot be disembedded from their social and political context. In this section we describe organizing principles and strategies that have emerged from one such group, the St. Thomas Resident Council (STRC) of the St. Thomas public housing development in New Orleans.

The St.Thomas housing development, which opened in 1941, is one of the oldest public housing developments in the United States. Public housing was segregated in its beginning and St.Thomas was built for whites. Originally St. Thomas was integrated into its neighborhood, but with the extension built in 1949, the massiveness of the development overtook the neighborhood. The entire development is 49.33 acres and consists of 1510 units. After desegregation the first black family moved into St.Thomas in 1965; today St.Thomas is 96 percent African-American (Calvert 1990).

As of May 1990 there were 4772 persons living in St.Thomas. Only 7 percent of the population is over twenty years old. Seventy percent is under fourteen. Ninety percent of the householders are female. Eighty-five percent have incomes below $15,000 and 61 percent have incomes lower than $5000 a year. Eighty-five percent receive some form of public assistance (Jones 1993).

The neighborhood in which St.Thomas sits, the St.Thomas/Irish Channel neighborhood, is a community of vast contrasts: wealthy whites live side-by-side with African-American poor; urban gentrification and renewal coexist with decaying housing. Thirty-four percent of the neighborhood residents have incomes under $5000, while seven percent have incomes between $50,000 and $100,000, and 2 percent have incomes over $100,000. A variety of social service agencies and homeowner and business associations coexist in the area (ULI 1993).

Since the late 1950s the St. Thomas development has been systematically cut off from the rest of the community in which it sits. What were originally through streets have been closed; escalating crime rates in the area have been used to stigmatize the residents as deviant; and social service delivery has largely been contained within the community. In more recent years, because of its prime location, St. Thomas has begun to experience the impact of encroaching development. First gentrification of the adjoining neighborhood, then riverfront development—from both the port, which is moving more of its terminals and warehouses away from the central business district and towards the St. Thomas area, and commercial development, especially as a result of pressures from riverboat gambling and the planned land-based casino (due to open in 1996). These development pressures are being experienced within a context that calls for the scaling back of public housing developments throughout the city, including St.Thomas (see Cook and Lauria 1993). There is much less discussion about where public housing residents would live, should the scale back occur. It is as a result of these kinds of encroachments that the women of St.Thomas have organized to resist urban development and maintain a space for themselves and their families.

The strategies of resistance described here have been driven by principles developed over a fifteen-year period as the St. Thomas residents worked in conjunction with the People's Institute for Survival and Beyond. The People's Institute conducts training programs nationwide centered around "Undoing Racism" for community organizers, social workers, and others interested in empowering people of color and poor communities. The training offers an "institutional power analysis" of racism which asserts that interlocking systems of social institutions surround poor communities and operate in a manner in which the accountability of institutional actors is to the institutions, rather than to the communities they serve. These institutions, it is argued, have been organized around implicit and explicit assumptions of white skin privilege and it is these assumptions that must be challenged if social and cultural change are to be brought about. The Institute works with community organizations in low-income communities of color to build self-determining, self-sufficient bases of community power that can obtain accountability from public and private social service organizations, as well as from political, educational, and economic institutions.

One of the organizers of the People's Institute is Barbara Major, who has been active in St.Thomas for the past fifteen years. She speaks of the need for a holistic approach to community development. At one level, holistic development strategies involve reintegrating the housing development back into the rest of the neighborhood. At another, holistic organizing seeks to reintegrate the members of the community who have been isolated from each other. This isolation stems from policies and programs that target particular sectors of the population for specific purposes:

> We develop programs holistically and what that means is that if we are dealing with families and those families have children or elders,[then] those children or elders are part of this community. When we deal with children then we understand

that those children are part of a cultural unit and that you cannot keep disenfranchising children from parents and families from community. You've got to look at the whole community in terms of what is good for the community and it plays itself out, if it's good for family, it's good for the community. (Interview with Barbara Major, May 1993)

The St. Thomas Residents Council (STRC) is a democratically organized body composed exclusively of low-income women of color who live in the St. Thomas development. Originally organized around housing issues, the residents' work developed into concern with institutionalized racism and economic well-being as it became clear to the members that housing, economics, and race oppression were inseparable. It is this recognition that gave rise to their holistic approach to community development.

In another example of holistic awareness, it is not feminist ideology but, rather, welfare and public housing policies that have constructed the group as exclusively female. These women are not engaged in the personal politics of gender. They understand that the spaces they inhabit are racially gendered because of the institutional organization that has been imposed upon their community. As Barbara Major states, "The thing about it [the Council] being all female is because black men have been deemed invisible in our community. There are so many policies that perpetuate that myth." These policies include federal housing policy (see Spain 1993) and welfare policy (see Abramovitz 1988), as well as practices engaged in by the police, the schools, and the medical profession. While the organization of the community is externally derived, the women are conscious of the restrictions imposed on them and the men in their families and are developing strategies to resist those restrictions. Thus men are encouraged to participate in the organizing activities initiated by the Council, and many men do, even though they do not sit on the Council.

What is clear for these women is that organizing their community is a many-faceted task. The work must go deeper than brick and mortar; it must reach into the fabric of the community to address internalized oppression as well as external control, exploitation, and paternalism. Doing this has meant working on many different fronts. STRC has organized an economic development corporation that will open its own dry goods store, a youth center committed to reducing teenage pregnancy, a neighborhood consortium made up of agency or institutional representatives and committed at-large individuals, and a partnership of land interests in the area that includes a major developer as well as many middle and upper-middle class property owners and their associations. In the remainder of this section we will discuss the ways that the principles of Undoing Racism guide an agenda of community self-determination, institutional accountability, and community building within the St. Thomas neighborhood.

It was necessary for the residents to define processes through which the community could empower itself to plan its own future. To do this required them to find ways to challenge the systems of power relations that provided for and regulated the community. Because so many low-income women depend upon the state and social service agencies for economic support, the first front of struggle on economic issues was with these institutions. That is, it is with those agencies that have the most immediate economic power over the community that residents first sought to empower themselves. For this reason the STRC worked to develop strategies for obtaining accountability from the institutions that surrounded their neighborhood.

In a letter sent to social service agencies and organizations serving St.Thomas residents, Barbara Jackson, the then-president of STRC, stated the council's demand for accountability:

> Historically, money dumped in the Black community without equal participation in the process has meant very little in terms of change. This ironically has not changed the attitude of the majority of agencies serving our community, they continually do what they perceive as being best for us. Proposals are written, monies received, and we are always left out of the process except to state in their proposals how pitiful we are, and how much we need them. . . . Therefore we accept no project that does not accept us as equal partners in the development of the project and its implementation. . . . If we can agree on equal respect, equal power in decision-making and equal sharing of resources, then we can proceed with developing an agenda. (Jackson, as cited in Jones 1993, 185–86)

Building an organizational structure that brings the various institutions together with the residents of the community they service is a long-term process, currently in its fifth year. In 1989 indigenous leaders of the St.Thomas Resident Council called together all social service agencies working within the St.Thomas area because they were tired of having these agencies speak on their behalf without input from the residents. As a result, the community representatives and social service agencies began meeting in open dialogue. In 1990 they formed the St.Thomas/Irish Channel Consortium. Accountable to the Resident Council, the Consortium consists of church-based organizations that have been in the neighborhood for many decades, advocacy groups including Planned Parenthood and Agenda for Children (the state's child advocacy agency which has its office in the neighborhood), medical clinics, and a university medical school which has programs in the neighborhood centered around child violence. The Board of Directors of the Consortium consists of representatives of these agencies, the People's Institute, as well as youth and at-large members. The Resident Council has veto power over all consortium board decisions. According to Fannie McKnight, vice president of the Resident Council, "This board is *the* board. We don't need any other boards in our neighborhood."

Long time St. Thomas activist and organizer Crystal Handy Jones (1993) has compiled a comprehensive case study which describes in detail the principles and processes of building the Consortium. According to Jones, the Consortium is based on an antiracist foundation.

> The indigenous community leaders mandated that the Consortium address as a priority the issue of racism and its impact on the community of color. . . . The indigenous leaders and community organizers were dealing with race more than just the issue of color variation—race was dealt with in terms of power. In fact, this community dealt with race in the context of power and institutional control. (Jones 1993, 2)

Thus, for these groups that have "come to the table," participation requires a commitment to support Undoing Racism and a willingness to accept the leadership of the Resident Council.

We observe that this has not always been an easy process but has required resolve on the part of the residents and the agency representatives. The Resident Council defines institutional accountability as a commitment to self-determination and liberation of oppressed people through cultural, political, and social change (Jones 1993). Such a commitment involves defining and implementing policy and delivering service in collaboration with the community. Putting that concept into actual practice within the agencies has been an ongoing process since the Consortium's inception. As Petrice Sams-Abiodun, a former resident of public housing who has completed a master's degree and is now coordinating a community-based program in St. Thomas, states:

> Service providers in this community are having to learn how to listen with different kinds of ears. They are having to learn how to listen to the voice of the community and to take direction from it. (Interview with Sams-Abiodun, August 1994)

During its existence the Consortium has been a forum for struggle and consciousness raising. It has also been a place to build a sense of community and extended family across race and class lines without ignoring the histories of oppression and privilege that underlie such relationships. We see here that the group has focused, as many other women-centered community development groups have, on developing workable processes for building partnership. By this, we observe that the focus of the group is not exclusively on building oppositional power to leverage or force accountability, but to build long-term relationships through committed struggle, even when the struggle is prolonged:

> One of our agencies really questioned the whole issue of accountability. We said, "You are either accountable, or you are not a part of, or you will not remain in this community." They weren't willing to leave and we weren't willing to uninvite them and we've struggled through on these issues. We've dialogued. We've talked and created the space to vent the anger for that oppressed community and the lack of understanding from the community that has the power and the resources. How do we do it and respect each other? The philosophy is that the consortium is a family and no one is prepared to leave. We will struggle through. That's what families do. (Interview with Barbara Major, May 1993)

As discussed above, the consortium and the collection of strategies implemented through it is part of the Resident Council's overall holistic approach to organizing that focuses upon process as political, and upon empowering individual members of the community as it addresses specific issues. The Kuji Center and Plain Talk are two programs developed by the Consortium to address issues of youth, especially issues related to teenage pregnancy and too-early sexuality. Both programs are community-based and seek to strengthen families so that they can better support their youth. The Kuji Center is a year-round, after-school program that seeks to improve and expand the life options available to teenagers in St. Thomas, and thus prevent teenage pregnancy. According to Demetria Farve, who is one of the mothers in St.Thomas and also the president of the Resident Council, "When I was a teenager sex seemed like the only recreation available to me. Now I'm 24 and I got four children. If there was Kuji when I was coming up I might have made different choices."

The Kuji Center was created in 1990, after the Consortium applied for and received a million dollar grant from a local foundation to create a community-based comprehensive service program that met the needs of the youth of St.Thomas. The Kuji Center responds to the needs of the teenagers by providing cultural, educational, and recreational programs, as well as entrepreneurship, leadership training, and peer counseling. The center's name is a shortened version of the Swahili word, *Kujichagulia*, which means "self-determination."

The Plain Talk initiative is funded by a national foundation to develop a community strategy for reaching sexually active teenagers. The foundation leaves specific programming to the community, but requires substantial ownership of the program among the residents. The St.Thomas leadership decided to use "home health parties" as a way of beginning a conversation in the community about how to protect sexually active youth. During the first year, over ninety parties were held, giving adults and youth an opportunity to explore in familiar surroundings issues of sexuality in general, as well as issues of domestic violence and child abuse.

Both the Kuji Center and Plain Talk seek to include men in their programming, and the efforts are beginning to pay off. For instance, at Plain Talk's initial retreat, no men showed up. At the retreat the following year, after a number of house parties during the year at which men were encouraged to take part in the discussions on sexuality, twelve men attended. The men and women have also used this time together to begin a discussion on violence in the community.

Our young men are talking about wanting to stop the violence in our community. They say they're tired of it. . . . We're taking a spiritual approach to dealing with all this violence. We're not crying and complaining, we're pulling ourselves up to fight. There's a spiritual grieving process going on. This city was dead but the people in this community is not. Shame can't be used against them anymore. (Interview with Fannie McKnight, May 23, 1994)

The Council is also involved in developing economic development strategies for the residents. For example, one current project involves the Resident Council opening a dry goods store in the neighborhood. The store will be operated by a council member and provide part-time employment for children of residents. The concept of the store was borrowed from another local community group that consulted with STRC as the Council developed its proposals and then sought out the resources to implement them. Many of the needed resources are in place for the store to open this year in a site turned over to STRC by the Housing Authority of New Orleans. It has taken a long time for the elements of the store to come together, but the slow progress has not concerned the organizer because she understands that the real emphasis is on balancing individual and collective empowerment, and changing the culture of the community.

The issue of siting the store is only one of many land-use concerns in the community. Land-use practices in St.Thomas are at the threshold of great flux. As Fannie McKnight has said, "Everybody over the years has been taking pieces of St.Thomas. . . . We've had developers coming from all over wanting this land. . . . They offered us jobs and apartments. It was all about the land." In response to the encroachment by the surrounding communities, the STRC over the last two years has helped to organize the Community Resource Partnership (CRP), whose aim is to achieve rehabilitation and restoration of St.Thomas and the surrounding area. In the CRP, residents have allied themselves with unlikely partners from within the community, including preservationists, upper-middle class homeowners and developers themselves:

> Gentrification and land speculation is our concern. We have formed another corporation in coalition with middle class homeowners near our area because they too are concerned with the specter of the casinos and the land development that seems to be headed towards us. We have unique alliances now with bankers, developers, and preservationists. It's got to go further than Rodney King's "Why can't we all just get along?" to "How are we going to get along?" We are addressing the inaccessibility of land to low-income people by addressing national land use policy. (Interview with Barbara Major, December 1993)

As part of its strategy the CRP has enlisted the assistance of the Urban Land Institute (ULI), a national nonprofit consulting firm. ULI conducted an intensive study of the St. Thomas community and developed a set of designs and recommendations aimed at revitalizing the entire neighborhood. These included opening up the now closed thoroughfares that segregate St. Thomas from the rest of the neighborhood, renovating the development, and turning it into a development with a mixture of residents from different socioeconomic levels. In other words, some renovated units would be rented to working-class families while others would continue to be leased to families on public assistance. At this time the CRP is involved in studying ULI's recommendations and in building the relational base to sustain the partnership and arrive at consensus in the STRC itself. The residents and the organizers know that this will not be an easy process, especially since developers and bankers are used to working with bricks and mortar, and not taking a holistic approach to development. But the slower approach is necessary because, as Barbara Major puts it, "We're not building a building. We're building an entire community and that takes time." The question that remains is that it is one thing to demand accountability from social service agencies but quite another to demand accountability from city hall and developers. From STRC's past experience with a developer who came into their community in the mid-1980s, Fannie McKnight knows how difficult and frustrating it can be. Speaking of that developer, Fannie McKnight says,

> He said he wanted [the land] because HUD wasn't going to invest in it. He said "I thought you people were going to take care of this." He meant the black elected officials were supposed to deal with us. He said that St.Thomas was a disgrace, that HUD shouldn't fund us and that we were a disgrace. He made it a racism situation. (Interview with Fannie McKnight, August 1994)

At the heart of STRC's work in CRP is the relationship they have built with a prominent developer who owns a large tract of riverfront land that lies between St.Thomas and downtown. Given that many low-income community organizations have traditionally had as much difficulty trusting developers as they have trusting public officials, we were curious as to what the basis of trust and accountability was with this developer. Central to this relationship was that the process began with a "straight up" acknowledgement of his goals and intentions:

> What impressed us was that he did not come to us with a charity mentality, "I want to help these po' people." He came to us and said "I'm a developer. I want to make money." And we said, "Right on, someone's coming in here trying to say it straight up" and we don't have a problem with that because folk are gonna make some money. We also want to make money and create jobs for the community. It's not about making the money, you can't make all the money and it can't be at our expense. (Interview with Barbara Major, December 1993)

As with the Consortium, this relationship has been built over time and is itself still evolving. What seems to be making this relationship work is the developer's willingness to embrace the resident's vocabulary for addressing the issues and to refrain from avoiding discussions of race and class differences:

> Trust has to be earned. This is not to say that things won't fall apart. You are always in a very vulnerable and tenuous relationship across such diverse lines but the trust has been earned in that he has worked with us in a respectful way. He has acknowledged the differences first of all. And has not tried to pretend that they are

not there. He's come to also see that there is a wisdom in [our] community that warrants listening to and following a lot of times. So far he's been honest and forthright about that and until he does otherwise we have no reason not to trust him. We're always wondering and I'm sure they're always wondering. People think that you just walk in and say "trust me." *But trust is an earned jewel and it comes through interacting and relationship building.* (Interview with Barbara Major, December, 1993; emphasis added)

This trust was not only built through the developer's rhetoric. He also brought the principles of STRC into practice in the course of his business. He has raised critical questions about a number of projects going on in the vicinity, questions that others in business would not expect a developer to raise. Such questions and other comments he has made lead the STRC to believe that he understands that his development plans will be more viable if their community is developed, too.

The development of a master plan for the neighborhood, the gathering of resources to implement it, and the actual revitalization of the community are sure to be lengthy processes. When considered in conjunction with the work of the consortium in bringing social service agencies to the table, the programs that support youth and their families, and the soon-to-be opened neighborhood store, it is clear that this holistic approach to organizing will keep the St.Thomas residents busy for some time to come. From the perspective of those organizing within St. Thomas, however, this time factor only guarantees that there will be lots of opportunities to build community. This community is inclusive of physical structures, collaborative policies and, most importantly, human relationships based on an acceptance of struggle and conflict, an appreciation of culture, and an ethic of accountability. It also holds a potential to "bleed up" into higher institutional levels, informing public and private policymaking and altering professional discourses such as the discourse of economic development we analyzed earlier.

Conclusions

This study of how low-income women of color organize to resist the impacts of urban restructuring on their lives extends our understanding of feminist theory in a number of ways. First, it helps us to see the role that public patriarchy (Sandercock and Forsyth 1992) directly plays in women's lives, and helps us redefine the nature and extent of the public domain. The move to privatize space, as a response to the crisis of restructuring, results in racially gendered space that is oppressive to men, as well as women, within low-income communities of color. Privatizing space fractures the city, creating fissures both within and between neighborhoods.

This study also reminds us that a multicultural analysis is important, for we cannot discuss the lives of women without the context of gender, race, and class (see Spelman 1988). Even among women, the city is experienced differently, depending on their race and class. For instance, the privatized enclosures are experienced as safe havens for middle-class white women; for lower-income black women, they represent an oppressive structure that requires their labor, takes resources out of their communities, and describes their men as objects of fear to be contained.

Working in conjunction with the People's Institute connects the community to a national network which is a larger scale discourse of resistance. It makes the experiential knowledge of organizers and activists from around the country available to inform and be informed by STRC's work. The People's Institute acts as a clearinghouse for dissemination of organizing knowledge and connects the community to a broad movement for antiracist social and cultural change.

The work of the St. Thomas Resident Council is a discourse of resistance through which the community is building alternative institutions and challenging existing ones to be accountable. They are resisting by changing the culture within the community: they are "throwing off" internalized oppression (i.e., creating another way of seeing themselves), and they are struggling with the powers that be to accept the community's definitions of itself. They are also working from a holistic approach rather than a piecemeal approach, which stands in contrast to traditional development practices. By engaging with developers, as well as policymakers in the context of accountability, the Council is challenging the unevenness of privilege and thus providing the possibilities of reintegrating racially gendered spaces into a more public, democratic whole.

References

Abramovitz, Mimi (1988). "Why Social Welfare is a Sham." *The Nation*, 247, 7: 221.
Acker, Joan (1992). "Gendered Institutions: From Sex Roles to Gendered Institutions." *Contemporary Sociology* 21 (September): 565–69.

Amott, Teresa L. (1990). "Black Women and AFDC: Making Entitlement out of Necessity." In Linda Gordon, ed. *Women, the State and Welfare*. Madison: University of Wisconsin Press, pp. 280-98.

Anzaldua, Gloria (1990). *Making Face, Making Soul= Haciendo Caras: Creative Critical Perspectives by Feminists of Color*. San Francisco: Aunt Lute Books.

Calvert, Linda (1990). "An Inquiry into the Feasibility of Community-Based Housing Strategies for the St.Thomas Neighborhood." A master's thesis presented to the faculty of the College of Urban and Public Affairs, University of New Orleans.

Cook, Christine C. and Mickey Lauria (1993). "Urban Regeneration and Public Housing in New Orleans." DURPS Working Paper # 17. New Orleans: Division of Urban Research and Policy Studies, University of New Orleans.

Crawford, Margaret (1992). "The World in a Shopping Mall." In Michael Sorkin, ed. *Variations on a Theme Park: The New American City and the End of Public Space*. New York: Hill and Wang. pp 3–30.

DuBois, Ellen Carol, and Vicki L. Ruiz (1990). *Unequal Sisters: A Multicultural Reader in U.S. Women's History*. New York: Routledge.

Dumm, Thomas L. (1993). "The New Enclosures: Racism in the Normalized Community." In Robert Gooding-Williams, ed. *Reading Rodney King/ Reading Urban Uprising*. New York:Routledge. pp 178–95.

Foucault, Michel (1980). *Power/Knowledge: Selected Interviews and Other Writings, 1972–1977*. Colin Gordon, ed. Brighton: Harvester Press.

Jones, Crystal Handy (1993). "The Bottom-Up Approach to Collaboration for Social Change: A Case Study of the St.Thomas/Irish Channel Consortium." A master's thesis presented to the faculty of the College of Urban and Public Affairs, University of New Orleans.

Kling, Joseph (1993). "Complex Society/Complex Cities: New Social Movements and the Restructuring of Urban Space." In Robert Fisher and Joseph Kling, eds. *Mobilizing the Community*. Newbury Park, CA: Sage, pp. 28–51.

Logan, John R. and Todd Swanstrom (1990). *Beyond the City Limits: Urban Policy and Economic Restructuring in Comparative Perspective*. Philadelphia: Temple University Press.

Mayer, M. (1991). "Politics in the post-Fordist City." *Socialist Review*. 21, pp. 105–24.

Ong, Aihwa (1987). *Spirits of Resistance and Capitalist Discipline: Factory Women in Malaysia*. Albany: State University of New York Press.

Sandercock, L. and A. Forsyth (1992). "A Gender Agenda: New Directions for Planning Theory." *APA Journal*, 58, pp.49–59.

Sassen, S. (1988). *The Mobility of Labor and Capital: A Study in International Investment and Capital Flow*. New York: Cambridge University Press.

Smith, Dorothy (1987). *The Everyday World as Problematic: A Feminist Sociology*. Boston: Northeastern University Press.

Spain, Daphne (1992). *Gendered Spaces*. Chapel Hill: University of North Carolina Press.

Spain, Daphne (1993). "Built to Last: Public Housing as an Urban Public Space." Paper presented at the Urban Affairs Association annual conference, Indianapolis, April 1993.

Spelman, Elizabeth V. (1988). *Inessential Woman: Problems of Exclusion in Feminist Thought*. Boston: Beacon Press.

Turner, Robyn S. (1993). "Concern For Gender In Central City Development Policy." Paper presented at the Urban Affairs Association Annual conference, Indianapolis, April 1993.

Urban Land Institute (1993). A presentation by the Urban Land Institute to the St.Thomas/Irish Channel Consortium, New Orleans, December 10, 1993.

5

Mixtecs and Mestizos in California Agriculture: Ethnic Displacement and Hierarchy among Mexican Farm Workers

Carol Zabin

In the last several years, the plight of America's farm workers has once again been in the public eye. Homelessness, poverty, exploitative work situations, and insecurity characterize the existence of many farm workers in this country. This dismal situation is in sharp contrast to the hopefulness of the late 1970s, when significant improvements in the living and working conditions of California farm workers were achieved. Unionization, the passage of protective legislation, and new social programs for migrant farm workers and their families all promised the end of the "farm worker problem" in the near future. Yet fifteen years later, conditions in the fields have deteriorated significantly. The improvements of the 1970s have not been consolidated; on the contrary, wages have fallen and livings conditions have worsened dramatically. The median yearly income of seasonal agricultural workers in the United States was between 5,000 and 7,500 dollars in 1989–90, and 62 percent of foreign-born farm workers live in poverty as defined by the U.S. census. (CIRS *Rural Report*, vol. 3, no. 3, 1990).

In the midst of these generally deteriorating conditions, another noteworthy change among California's farm workers has occurred. The farm labor force is being transformed from one traditionally dominated by mestizo Mexicans (of mixed European and Indian descent), who come from north-central Mexico, to one in which indigenous peasants from the southern states of Mexico comprise a growing proportion. The most predominant of the indigenous groups are Mixtec Indians from Oaxaca, one of the poorest states in Mexico.

Since the institution of the Bracero Program during World War II, a large majority of farm workers have been Mexican immigrants or their children. By 1983, 90 percent of all hired farm labor was Mexican or Mexican-American (Mines and Martin 1986). Today, for hand harvest and preharvest tasks in many crops in California the work force is exclusively Mexican nationals. However, Mexican farm workers are not a homogeneous group, and one important distiinction is that between mestizo and indigenous people.

Mestizo Mexican immigrants come from what is often called the traditional sending states of Mexico, where many villages have been sending migrants to work in U.S. agriculture since the Mexican Revolution at the beginning of this century (Massey et al. 1987). The social networks of migrants from these villages have acquired substantial collective experience and contacts in the United States that allow them to channel new villagers into jobs with relative ease. The "maturity" of these mestizo immigrant social networks gives their members a considerable advantage over migrants from new networks, such as the Mixtecs from Oaxaca.

In contrast, the Mixtecs and other indigenous farm workers are more recent migrants, more of them are undocumented and many do not speak Spanish, much less English. Moreover, indigenous people in general and Mixtecs in particular come from the poorest areas of Mexico, where access to education and health care is limited, and 500 years of ethnic oppression still shape their daily lives (Varese 1985, 1986; Warman 1984). Poverty at home affects the migration experience as well. Migrating with fewer resources and greater need at home, and travelling longer distances than their counterparts from the traditional sending areas, Mixtecs face the California labor market from a more vulnerable position than most mestizo workers.

This article suggests that Mixtecs are playing a key role in the current deterioration of conditions in the farm labor market because access to this work force gives employers the opportunity to lower their harvesting costs. In fact, the incorporation of Oaxacans into the California farm labor market is the latest phase of the recurrent cycle of ethnic succession that has made improvements in the farm labor market infrequent and temporary. Since the late 1800s, when labor-intensive fruit and vegetable production took hold in California, the state's farm labor history has been characterized by the sequential entry of groups of foreign workers: farm workers have been successively Chinese, Japanese, Filipinos, "okies" and "arkies," before they were mestizo or indigenous Mexicans. Except at the height of the Great Depression, white U.S. citizens have never measured more than a small portion of California farm labor, and an even smaller part when only field hands are included (Fisher 1953; McWilliams 1979).

The process of ethnic succession has followed a relatively similar pattern for each immigrant group. Historically, as each immigrant group settled in California, its members fought for, and sometimes gained, better wages and working conditions. Unionization efforts, ethnic associations or other forms of farm worker organization have played key roles in the life cycle of every immigrant farm worker group in California's history (McWilliams 1979; Fisher 1953). In fact, it has been most often in response to the pressures for improvements in wages and working conditions brought about by workers' collective action that employers have sought new immigrants groups to replace them or otherwise undermine their bargaining power (McWilliams 1979; Galarza 1964). Thus historically, employers have gained access to new foreign groups that could be brought in for lower wages, eroding the gains of previous generations of farm workers. Over the last one hundred years, the only farm workers who have been able to improve their economic status significantly have been those who could move up and out of farm work. Improvements in the farm labor market itself have never been sustained.

This study analyzes recent transformations in the farm labor market in California by examining the effect on farm worker wages and working conditions of (1) the changing macro-economic conditions, specifically the deepening integration of Mexican and United States fruit and vegetable production on farm worker wages and conditions; and (2) the changing composition of the labor force as Mixtec migrants begin to substitute for mestizo Mexican workers.

The study first documents the current cycle of ethnic succession by documenting the gains of the United Farm Workers era and analyzing the reasons for the reversal of those gains. Next, the current wages and working conditions of the Mixtecs are documented and compared to other farm workers in California. The following section presents an

ethnographic analysis of the nature of the competition for jobs between indigenous and mestizo workers and the effect this has on the
wages, incomes, and working conditions of farm workers in California. Finally, conclusions and policy implications are presented.

The study is based on a survey of Mixtec farm workers carried out
by the author and her field assistant in California and Oregon in 1990
and 1991. Interviews were conducted with 129 Mixtec field workers,
yielding detailed work and migration histories as well as demographic
and occupational information about migrants' families. Random sampling was not possible because the Mixtec population is very mobile,
and no clear population universe could be identified. Moreover, a
large number of the Mixtecs interviewed were undocumented. To over-
come the difficulty of finding Mixtec workers, researchers worked
with a team of anthropologists, social workers and Mixtec community
leaders to snowball sample Mixtecs. The survey was conducted mainly
in California's San Joaquin Valley, home to the majority of settled
Mixtecs in the United States. A small number of interviews were
carried out in the Willamette Valley of Oregon, where seasonal Mixtec
migrants harvest berries in early summer and then return to California
or Mexico. To avoid the bias in a snowball sample limited to one
migrant social network, workers from thirty-six villages in Oaxaca
were interviewed, with no village represented by more than twelve
workers.

Labor Relations in California Agriculture: 1965–1992

Improvements in conditions for California farm workers were set
into motion soon after 1964, when the Bracero Program was terminated under tremendous political pressure by labor unions and civil
rights leaders (Jenkins 1985). The Bracero Program was a contract
workers program administered by the Mexican and U.S. government
to provide seasonal workers to growers in the United States. Labor
rights advocates argued that the program undermined the ability of
farm workers in the United States by providing temporary workers
who were not granted the same legal rights and labor standards as
other workers in this country. The following year, the National Farm
Workers Association joined forces with the AFL-CIO's Agricultural
Workers Organizing Committee (AWOC) in organizing the famous
Delano grape strike. In 1966, these two groups formed the United

Farm Workers of America (Majka and Majka 1982). Over the following fifteen years, widespread mobilization of workers and national
political organizing resulted in significant improvements in conditions
for California farm workers.

The gains of the United Farm Workers (UFW) were substantial in
at least four important arenas: improvements in wages and working
conditions, the passing of legislation protecting the legal rights of farm
workers, the creation of social programs specifically designed for farm
workers, and dramatic changes in the political culture of rural California as Mexican immigrants and Mexican Americans began to voice
their concerns in public and political arenas.

By 1970, the UFW had negotiated collective bargaining contracts
with 150 ranches, representing 10,000 workers (Majka and Majka
1982). By 1973, union contracts covered 40,000 jobs, mostly in grapes
and lettuce, but including altogether forty different crops in 500 different locations in California. The UFW was the first farm labor union
that successfully organized throughout the state of California. Although
probably no more than 15 percent of the agricultural work force was
ever under union contract, the influence of the UFW extended far
beyond actual contracts (Lloyd et al 1988). The UFW was such a
threat to some growers that they anxiously signed contracts with the
Teamsters, in order to quell support for the more radical union (Martin
1989). Other groups of growers also tried to avoid unionization by
unilaterally improving wages, benefits, and working conditions for
their workers (Martin and Lloyd). For the first time, farm workers in
at least three of the most important regions of California, Ventura
County, the Imperial Valley, and the Salinas Valley, gained significant
improvements in wages and won rights to seniority, vacation pay, sick
leave, medical insurance, and grower-provided family housing (Mines
and Anzaldua 1982; Martin 1989; Villarejo 1989). By 1983, wages for
unionized farm workers averaged $5.54 per hour, while nonunion farm
workers earned only $4.46 per hour (Martin 1989).

In 1975, the United Farm Workers and other activist groups lobbied
successfully for passage of the California Agricultural Labor Relations
Act, which for the first time extended to farm workers the right to
collective bargaining and union representation. This was hailed as a
major victory for farm labor (Wells and West 1989). Other legislation
was passed during this period, granting farm workers the California
minimum wage (1961 for women and children, 1967 for men), unem-

ployment insurance (1976) and Workers' Compensation (1976) and other protections that had previously been available only to workers in other sectors of the economy.

In addition, many social programs were created especially to meet the needs of farm workers, including Migrant Education for the children of migrant farm workers, the state-wide system of rural health clinics, and the state-run family labor camps. The family labor camps, for example, not only provided a significant subsidy to household income and allowed families to stay together, but also incorporated a management structure with a democratically elected governing body designed to encourage organization and participation. The rural health clinics and the legal aid agency created specifically for farm workers, California Rural Legal Assistance, also had community advisory boards to assure representation of their client population in policy decisions. These social programs thus provided new mechanisms with which to foster the growing political activism of farm workers.

A vital legacy of the movement spearheaded by Cesar Chavez was a change in the political culture of California, which has taken on growing significance as the demographic composition of California becomes more dominated by Mexicans and Mexican-Americans. The United Farm Workers inspired and shaped the lives of an entire generation of Mexican-Americans, producing leaders of the Chicano movement, artists, and other activists and professionals who to this day are important players in California politics (Cruz and Avila 1989). One of the most significant changes in rural California is the substantial success of Hispanic elected officials in rural farm workers towns that had been previously controlled by farmers (ibid). A surprising number of these elected officials are former UFW organizers (ibid).

The Deterioration of Conditions for Farm Workers in the 1980s

By virtually every indicator, there has been a sharp reversal in the improvements in wages and working conditions for farm workers described above over the 1980s. Wages in California agriculture have declined significantly over the last ten years. The United Farm Workers has lost influence and has currently very few workers under union contract. Some new small unions have sprouted up, but each has only a handful of contracts in isolated areas. Overall, only a few thousand workers are now under any kind of union contract (Runsten 1991).

According to government data, real wages for farm workers aggregated over all crops declined almost 10 percent, while wages in manufacturing fell at only about half the rate of farm labor (CIRS 1990). In some crops, such as raisin grapes, they have declined 40 percent (CIRS, 1990).[1]

For farm workers, wages are often not the most important indicators of changes in real net income and welfare. A major difficulty for farm workers is the seasonality of agricultural jobs and the difficulty of splicing together a yearly job circuit. Unfortunately, there is no reliable data to measure changes in unemployment in this sector over the last ten years. There is clearly a labor surplus in California, as evidenced from case studies, and the recently released Commission on Agricultural Workers evaluation of Special Agricultural Workers Program of the 1986 Immigration Reform and Control Act (*New York Times* October 22, 1992; Runsten et al. 1992; Martin 1992). Fringe benefits have virtually disappeared in the last ten years. Much of the housing previously provided by growers has also been eliminated (Runsten 1991a).

Workers are bearing more and more of the costs associated with the seasonal nature of agriculture. Even during the Bracero Program, which has generally been characterized as a period of severe restrictions on workers rights (Galarza 1964), workers were provided housing and guaranteed a minimum number of work days per season. In contrast, the chaos and destabilization that characterizes the farm labor market today results in very high job search costs for workers, great uncertainty, and substantial degrees of homelessness. Under current conditions in the farm labor market, the grower pays none of the costs associated with guaranteeing the availability of a labor force during an often critically short harvesting season. The grower can, as many farm labor advocates say, hire and fire workers as easily as turning on and off a water spigot.

Paralelling other sectors of the U.S. economy, farm union membership and activity in California has declined dramatically over the last ten years. The UFW has lost influence and currently has very few workers under union contract. Some new, small unions have sprouted up, but each has only a handful of contracts in isolated areas. Overall, less than 10,000 workers are now under any kind of union contract in California, where over 500,000 farm workers are employed.[2]

Employment of workers by farm labor contractors has increased dramatically, rising by 74 percent in the 1978–87 period, another indicator of deteriorating conditions for California farm workers (Villarejo

1989, Martin 1989). Farm labor contractors are entrepreneurs who recruit, transport, and supervise crews, take care of pay rolls, tax deductions, and sometimes house and feed workers, and who bridge the language and cultural gap between many employers and their workers. They ordinarily contract with growers and packing houses to provide crews at specified costs and time, thus eliminating the need for growers to carry out the variety of tasks associated with managing their labor force. Unemployment insurance data in California show contractors paying from 50-75 percent of state average farm wages, depending on the region (Vaupel and Martin 1986). Farm labor contractors also pay lower social costs because undocumented workers are disproportionately employed by them: Unemployment insurance taxes are lower because undocumented workers cannot apply for benefits, and worker's compensation taxes are lower because injuries are often not reported by the undocumented who fear detection and deportation.

Structural Changes Leading to the Deterioration of the Farm Labor Market

The inability of the United Farm Workers to consolidate improvements in the farm labor market has multiple causes. The discussion here is limited to the structural changes that made it difficult for this low-skilled work force to protect itself from downward pressures on wages, although internal problems in the United Farm Workers also played a role.[3]

The transnationalization of California agriculture poses new structural challenges to efforts to improve conditions for farm workers. Economic crisis and structural adjustment in Mexico have propelled new waves of U.S.-bound migration and at the same time attracted United States agricultural capital to Mexico, which has become a chief competitor of California produce over the last ten years. These twin outcomes of the deepening economic links between rural Mexico and rural California have undermined the bargaining position of workers vis-à-vis employers in the California farm labor market, the first by creating a situation of surplus labor, and the second by creating pressure on growers in California to reduce costs. As discussed later, the recruitment of Mixtecs by growers in northwest Mexico, and their subsequent migration across the border, provides a revealing example of how production and labor flows between the United States are linked.

Expansion of Mexican Horticultural Exports

California agriculture was the leading producing region for the fresh fruit and vegetable market in the United States until the mid-1970s, when other regions both within the United States and in other parts of the world began to increase their market share (Runsten and Chalfont 1988). California fresh and frozen broccoli, cauliflower, strawberries, and fresh tomatoes now face significant competition from Mexico. Although continued growth in demand for fresh fruits and vegetables has allowed production in California to expand moderately in most crops, competition makes California growers especially cost-conscious (ibid).

The state of Sinaloa in Mexico had became an important supplier of fresh produce for the U.S. winter market in the late 1960s, replacing Cuba as a destination for U.S. agribusiness investment. As real wages fell and the peso devalued during the 1980s, horticulture exports from Sinaloa increased, and Sonora and Baja California also rapidly expanded horticultural exports (ibid). Growers on both sides of the border sell fruits and vegetables through the same marketing channels to the same markets, use very similar production technologies, belong to the same U.S. trade associations, and even use the same USDA agricultural extension services (Cook and Amon 1988; Runsten et al. 1993; Zabin and Hughes, 1993).

Thus, even before the passage of the North American Free Trade Agreement (NAFTA), the horticultural sector on both sides of the border was highly integrated. The expansion of horticultural production is expected to continue during NAFTA's phased-in reduction of tariffs, but to a great extent, rationalization of production has already taken place (Runsten and Wilcox 1992). Clearly, competition with Mexican production heightens pressures to lower wages on the U.S. side.

Increased Mexican Migration

Accelerating migration during the 1980s has allowed California growers to respond to competitive pressures by lowering labor costs. When farmers have access to large numbers of new migrants whose economic need forces them to accept lower wages, unionized workers have little ability over the long run to protect the gains they won through collective bargaining.

TABLE 1
Border Apprehensions

Year	Arrests of undocumented foreigners by U.S. Border Patrol along entire U.S.-Mexican border
1982	743,830
1983	1,034,142
1984	1,056,907
1985	1,185,795
1986	1,615,854*
1987	1,112,067
1988	943,063
1989	854,939
1990	1,103,353
1991	1,132,933

*Fiscal 1986 was the year preceding passage of the Immigration Reform and Control Act.

Undocumented immigration from Mexico increased dramatically in the 1980s in response to Mexico's economic crisis. Table 1 shows the increase in apprehensions of undocumented workers by the U.S. Border Patrol. Although faulty as a measure of the entry of undocumented workers, this data gives some indication of the sharp increase of illegal entries in the early 1980s.[4]

The number of apprehensions dropped dramatically in 1987, after the Immigration Control and Reform Act (IRCA)[5] was passed, but has been on the rise again and is now approaching pre-IRCA levels.

Moreover, agricultural employers were able to influence the content of the 1986 Immigration Reform and Control Act by creating a special provision applicable only to the agricultural sector. During the debates on immigration reform, agricultural employers lobbied unsuccessfully for a new contract labor or "guest worker" program, which would create a special farm labor force not subject to the same labor legislation as citizen workers. This was unacceptable to farm labor advocates. The political compromise that was reached instead was the Special Agricultural Workers provision within the 1986 IRCA, known as the SAW program. This program allowed workers who had worked ninety days in agriculture between May 1985 and May 1986 to obtain residency.[6]

In essence the SAW program functioned to recruit workers, since both employers and immigrant advocates helped thousands of workers obtain documents. This led to a one-time increase in the supply of farm labor. In California alone, 700,000 people applied for amnesty under the SAW provision, about 50 percent more than the entire estimated farm work force in the state (Martin 1989).[7]

Somewhat ironically, then, many scholars have concluded that IRCA has stimulated rather than slowed continued migration from Mexico (Runsten 1991; Cornelius 1992), or at the very least demonstrate that IRCA has not been able to deter decisions to migrate (Donato and Massey 1990). The law's major loophole is that it does not require employers to check the veracity of documents. The use of fraudulent documents is a normal and accepted fact of life for both employers and workers (Cornelius 1992). While employers were not able to design immigration law unilaterally because the political process required compromise and negotiation, the SAW provision has in practice been favorable for them. It has essentially guaranteed farmers continual replenishment of their work force by new migrant workers who are propelled from their home country by economic necessity.

Ethnic Hierarchies in the California Farm Labor Market

The expansion of the horticulture sector in Northwest Mexico over the last fifteen years has also changed the ethnic composition of the farm labor force in California, by putting into motion new migration flows of indigenous people from southern Mexico. Growers in Sinaloa, Sonora and Baja recruited and provided free transport for workers from southern Mexico, regions of high poverty and unemployment. Growers purposely recruited in regions where established U.S. migration flows did not exist, believing that they would have difficulty retaining a work force that already had experience crossing the border and working in the United States (Zabin and Hughes 1995). Indigenous Mixtecs from the state of Oaxaca were the largest group recruited in this fashion by growers in Northwest Mexico.

The Mixteca region of Oaxaca is one of the poorest in all Mexico, with high levels of malnutrition, high mortality rates, and low literacy and education levels. Soil degradation in the region is very advanced, and maize yields average less than 500 kilograms per hectare, way below the national average. Other economic activities in the region include the raising of goats, artesanry, and some logging and coffee production, but none of these provides sufficient employment or income to retain the work force.

The region has experienced very high rates of outmigration for over fifty years. Mixtecs had migrated to the United States during the Bracero program, but unlike mestizo migrants from central Mexico, most discontinued U.S. migration after the program ended. They apparently faced more difficulties in migrating than their mestizo counterparts because of high levels of monolinguism and fewer beachhead contacts that could give them access to employers once the government-run program was terminated.[8]

Many Mixtecs were instead recruited to work in the agro-export fields of northern Mexico. Wage labor first in Sinaloa, and later in Baja, provided an alternative to low-yield subsistence agriculture in Oaxaca. Employers continue to send buses to the isolated highland region of Mixteca, providing free transport and food for the trip north, and free, albeit substandard housing while they are employed.

In the late 1970s and early 1980s, Mixtecs again started migrating to the United States, aided by the contacts they made in Sinaloa and Baja and their now greater proximity to California (Kearney 1986; Zabin and Hughes 1995). Sixty-seven percent of the Mixtecs interviewed in the California and Oregon had worked in Baja before they got jobs in the United States (Zabin et al. 1993). An estimated 20,000 to 30,000 thousand Mixtecs are in California in the peak months of the agricultural cycle (Runsten et al. n.d.).

Demographic Features and the Labor Market Experience of Mixtecs in California

Table 2 presents basic demographic information about the Mixtec workers interviewed in California and Oregon. The Mixtec data are compared to two other farm worker surveys, whenever data is available. The first survey was carried out under the auspices of the California Employment Development Division (EDD) by Alvarado et al. in 1990. This survey selected a random sample of employers from Fresno, Kern, Madera, and Tulare counties in the San Joaquin Valley in California and interviewed 347 workers working in these firms. The second survey is the California component of the National Agricultural Workers Survey (henceforth called the NAWS data), a 1989 and 1990 survey financed by the U.S. Department of Labor as mandated by the IRCA legislation. Since neither survey asked the ethnicity of the farm workers they interviewed, no information is available to indicate whether or not Mixtecs were among those surveyed. If they were, presumably they were included in the sample in proportion to their

TABLE 2
Demographic Characteristics of Mixtec and Other Farmworkers 1989–90

	Mixtec Sample	EDD San Joaquin Valley Sample	NAWS
Age (mean)	29.5	34.9	34
% Female	13.0	27.7	26
Immigration Status:			
Undocumented	34.8	6.8	9
SAW	59.1	42.6	62
Documented through other programs	3.8	51.6	29
Yrs. since first came to U.S. (mean)	7.2	12.7	12
Yrs. education	4.1	5.9	6
% married	61.4	62.3	66
% whose fathers were farm laborers	52.7	79.8	n.a.
% whose fathers were small farmers in Mexico	32.1	n.a.	n.a.
% whose mothers were farm laborers	22.1	22.3	n.a.

Source: Mixtec Survey; Alvarado, et al. 1990; NAWS, 1993

numbers in the area surveyed, and thus consist of representative samples of all farm workers, including Mixtecs. Finally, information published by the California EDD from their records on unemployment insurance (henceforth called the EDD UI data), is also used when no direct information from worker surveys is available.

Table 2 demonstrates that the Mixtec migrants are on average younger and have fewer years of education than other farm workers in California. In fact, only fifteen percent of the Mixtecs have more than six years of education, and fifty percent have three or fewer years of education. This is lower than the average for the Mexican population as a whole, and reflects the early entry of many Mixtec workers into the migrant work circuit within Mexico, especially in Sinaloa and Baja California. Many of those interviewed said they began to work in the agribusiness fields of Northern Mexico when they were eight or nine years old.

As noted earlier, Mixtecs are a relatively new group of migrants in California. The mean number of years since a Mixtec worker entered the country was 7.2 compared with means from the NAWS and EDD

TABLE 3
Wage Comparisons
Mixtec and EDD Unemployment Insurance Data

| | Mixtec | EDD U.I. | |
	Mean Wages 1990	Mean Wages, Jan. 1991	Mean Wages, Dec. 1990
Vegetables & Melons	$4.91	$6.34	$6.95
Grapes	5.23	5.93	6.08
Deciduous fruit	4.77	5.60	5.35
Other	4.36	6.29	5.61
Total fruit and tree nuts	5.01	5.98	6.95

Source: Mixtec Survey; EDD 1991, Table 1-E.

surveys of twelve and thirteen years, respectively. Only eight percent of the Mixtec workers came to the United States before 1976.[9]

A significantly high proportion of the Mixtecs are undocumented: over one-third of all the Mixtecs interviewed working without legal papers, compared with less than 10 percent of the workers in the EDD and NAWS survey, as shown in table 2. Fifty-nine percent of the Mixtecs obtained documents under the SAW provision of IRCA, indicating that until 1987, nearly all Mixtec workers in the United States were undocumented.

Wages

The survey of Mixtec workers collected detailed wage and employment data for four jobs in which the worker worked in 1989–90.[10]

Average wages across all crops are considerably lower for Mixtec workers than for workers sampled in the NAWS survey: Mixtec average wages were $4.82 per hour while the equivalent for the NAWS workers was $5.41.[11]

Neither the NAWS nor San Joaquin studies published wage data disaggregated by crop for California. Table 3 compares the disaggregated wage data from the Mixtec survey with the only available data series by crop type, that calculated by California EDD from the wages reported to them through employment tax records, herein called the EDD UI data.[12] The table shows that in every category, the Mixtecs have mean hourly wage earnings significantly lower than the statewide sample.

The wage data from the Mixtec survey shows the widespread violation of minimum wage laws by growers employing this group of work-

TABLE 4
Wages of Mixtecs by crops and tasks

	Mean hourly wage equivalent	% earning less than minimum wage	Number of reports
Rasberry harvest, Oregon	$3.72	64	11
Strawberry harvest, Oregon	4.74	39	31
Cucumber harvest, Oregon	4.81	42	12
Tomato harvest, San Joaquin Valley, Calif.	5.69	10	10
Grape pruning, San Joaquin Valley, Calif.	4.27	30	40
Raisin grape harvest, San Joaquin Valley, Calif.	5.29	30	32
Table grape harvest, San Joaquin Valley, Calif.	5.80	50	10
Wine grape harvest, San Joaquin Valley, Calif.	5.60	33	6
Cotton hoeing and thinning	4.50	0	15
Olive harvest, Northern Calif.	4.36	33	6
Garlic Harvest, San Joaquin and Salinas Valleys	5.41	33	9

Source: Mixtec survey

ers, as illustrated in Table 4. Although the mean wages over all workers in each crop consistently were above the minimum wage, one third of the workers in the sample earned less than the minimum hourly wage.

In the Mixtec sample, 64.5 percent of the current jobs were paid on a piece rate basis, while 33.1 percent were paid by the hour and 2.4 percent were paid on some other basis. Most of the violation of minimum wage standards occured in work that is paid on a piece rate basis even though the law clearly states that workers must earn at least the equivalent of the minimum wage when paid by piece rate. Only a handful of workers report earning less than the minimum wage when paid on an hourly or daily basis; presumably because it is much easier to verify minimum wage violations when workers are paid by the hour.

One explanation for low wages of piece-rate workers is the possible lower productivity of Mixtec workers. Unfortunately, there are currently no comparable data sets to measure the volume produced of other workers in the same crops. Moreover, since conditions in fields

TABLE 5
Work Patterns of Mixtecs and
San Joaquin Valley EDD Farmworkers

	Mixtec	EDD	NAWS
Worked outside the county where they were interviewed	83.0%	40.0%	n.a.
Worked for current employers in 1988	65.0%	61.0%	n.a.
Average number of farm work jobs per worker in 1988	6.5	2.7	n.a.
Number of months in farm work	4.8	4.63	7.56

Source: Mixtec Survey; Alvarado, et al. 1990; NAWS, 1993.

vary, it is extremely difficult to compare productivities even if information about the volume produced by different groups were available. However, all anecdotal evidence suggests that the Mixtecs are at least as productive as other workers. Many growers praised their speed and agility. In words similar to those used by their predecessors to describe the Chinese and Japanese workers when they first began working as farm laborers and conformed to growers needs as cheap and compliant workers (Jones 1970), growers and farm labor contractors often commented about how the Mixtecs were especially well suited for farm work due to their short stature and agile hands.

Work Patterns

Table 5 compares the employment patterns in the Mixtec and other California farm workers surveys. The Mixtecs were much more migratory than workers in the EDD sample: whereas only forty percent of the EDD workers travelled outside their county of residence to work, 83 percent of the Mixtecs did so. Table 6 shows the large distances that Mixtecs travel to find work. Only 18 percent of the Mixtecs worked exclusively in the state of California, while many traveled between Oregon, California and/or Mexico each year.

Another significant difference in employment patterns is the number of farm work jobs that the Mixtec have per year (6.5) compared to the EDD sample of farm workers (2.7), also documented in table 5. This difference in the number of jobs cannot be explained by a longer total duration of farm work employment for the Mixtec sample, since

TABLE 6
Yearly Job Circuit
Percent of Mixtecs working in various regions in 1989–90

California only	California and the Northwest (Oregon and/or Washington)	California, the Northwest and Mexico	California and Mexico	Other
17	18	20	25	20

the total number of months that Mixtecs, on average, spend in farm work is only slightly higher than that of the EDD San Joaquin sample. Instead, it reflects the concentration of Mixtec workers in jobs that have very short seasons. Since job search costs are generally quite high in farm work, involving significant transportation costs and uncertainty, the marked seasonality of the Mixtecs' work is especially significant.[13]

Benefits

Mixtec workers also are concentrated in farm work jobs that have few benefits. In general, farm work jobs provide very few benefits, and there has been a significant decrease in benefits for farm workers over the last ten to fifteen years (Martin 1989, Runsten 1991). Table 7 shows that while a quarter and a third of the workers in the EDD San Joaquin and NAWS surveys, respectively, receive health insurance, only one Mixtec worker in the entire Mixtec sample was eligible for this benefit. Other farm workers are also much more likely to receive paid vacation, again, only one Mixtec worker did.

The Farm Labor Contractor System and Obligatory Services

The Mixtec data confirm that workers employed by farm labor contractors earn less than workers employed directly by growers. However, there was no significant difference between the *average hourly wages* (including the hourly equivalent for piece-rate workers) of Mixtecs employed by FLCs and those employed by growers. The difference in net income arose because of the difference in benefits and charges accompanying the two types of employers. These differences are shown in Table 8.

TABLE 7
Benefits and Charges
Mixtec and other California Surveys

	Mixtec	EDD	NAWS
Workers who are covered by health insurance	0.3%	25.1%	32%
Workers who received paid vacation	0.3%	6.5%	15%
Workers who pay employer for transport to work	31.4%	21.0%	n.a.
Average daily charge for transport to work	$3.66	$2.99	n.a.

Source: Mixtec Survey; Alvarado, et al. 1990; NAWS, 1993.

The most significant disadvantage of working for a farm labor contractor occurs when workers are obligated to purchase transport, housing, food, or equipment services from the *mayordomo* or contractor as a condition of employment. These tied labor arrangements extract income from the workers wage by requiring them to purchase these services at above market rates. In the San Joaquin Valley, a prevalent tied labor arrangement is the *raitero* system. Under this system, workers obtain work through their crew boss or *mayordomo*, who give them a ride to work (hence the name *"raitero"*) in their van or bus. The transport service costs each worker between $3.00 and $6.00 a day and *is a condition of employment*. A worker is not allowed to use his own car or carpool if he wants a job with this crew. Workers who paid transport charges to friends or co-workers rather than to employers or supervisors paid an average of $2.46 per day compared to an average of $3.66 paid to *raiteros*. Table 7 suggests that Mixtecs not only pay on average a higher charge for transport, but are more likely to work in jobs that charge workers for transportation.

Nonpayment of Wages

The Mixtec survey asked workers if they had ever experienced nonpayment of wages for work in the United States. This is one of the most serious of all labor standards violations, and can be taken as an indication of the depth and breadth of labor standards violations by employers of Mixtecs. Twenty-six percent of the Mixtecs interviewed said they had been refused payment on at least one job since they had been working in the United States. The amount they were owed by employers varied from $50 to $1,500. While there is no way to verify these claims, interviews with attorneys for California Rural Legal Assistance (CRLA) and leaders of the Mixtec organizations lend cre-

TABLE 8
Wage, Transport, and Housing Differentials for Mixtecs employed
by Farm Labor Contractors and Growers

(averages)	ALL MIXTECS (n=57)	Hired by FLCs	Hired by growers
Hourly wages (a)	$4.87	$4.86	$4.89
Daily wages (b)	37.73	37.56	37.88
Daily cost of transport (c)[1]	1.57	2.26	.85
% paying employer for transport	28%	41%[2]	14%
Daily rent (d)[1]	2.10	3.62	.73
% paying rent	49%	66%	30%
NET DAILY WAGE (e)[3]	$34.06	$31.68	$36.20

1. Averages include those who pay nothing. The average cost of a *raite* was $3.66.
2. In the entire sample, 49 percent of the Mixtecs working for an FLC paid their employer for a *raite*.
3. (e) = (b) – (c) – (d)
Source: Mixtec Survey

dence to the responses from the survey. Gloria Hernandez, of the Fresno California Rural Legal Assistance office, described the labor standards violations her office has dealt with:

> [W]ith respect to the many [labor standards violoations] cases of Mixtecs that we've had, all of them have arisen from wage claims. There weren't any claims for minimum wage violations or because they haven't been paid overtime, but rather because they haven't been paid at all. This is very different than for the workers from places like Michoacan, Texas, and Monterrey, who not only fight for their wages, but also benefits, housing, unemployment insurance, etc. The Mixtecs don't do this, they just fight for their wages, what's owed to them. (Cited in Zabin 1992, 33)

Job Competition between Mestizos and Mixtecs

The evidence is strong that Mixtecs work under poorer conditions than the typical mestizo Mexican farm worker. In the introduction, we hypothesized that their entry also has had repercussions for the farm labor market as a whole. This is a similar question to one commonly addressed by immigration scholars: to what extent do workers born in the United States experience displacement and wage depression as a consequence of immigration? Clearly, the entry of Mixtecs has had little effect on native-born farm workers in California, since the work force is over 90 percent foreign born. However, the entry of Mixtecs can impact longtime settled mestizo Mexican immigrants.

Analysis of the impact of the entry of a new group of workers on the wages and employment levels of native-born workers is complex because it ideally should encompass both issues of job competition between groups of workers and other economy-wide effects such as demand side multiplier effcts and the long-term effects of immigration on income growth (see Greenwood and McDowell 1990; Borjas 1990; Bean et al. 1988; Piore 1979). Two general approaches have been taken to study this issue, case studies of specific sectors documenting changes in work forces and working conditions over time, and econometric tests of cross-sectional data on cities with different proportions of immigrants (see Bach 1984 for examples of the former, and Borjas 1990 for examples of the latter). Frequently, case studies show significant negative effects of immigrants on native-born minority populations, while cross-sectional tests show little or no effect. Both methodologies have limitations. Case studies cannot capture the effects of immigration that extend beyond the sector they study and thus miss the stimulation to economic growth that immigration entails via demand side multipliers. Econometric tests have been faulted because they attempt to simulate a process that occurs over time without real data on the specific set of workers affected by immigrant recruitment into an industry.[14]

This paper follows the case study methodology and presents ethnographic evidence of displacement and wage depression. The evidence shows that in some cases, mestizo workers are losing their jobs as growers replace them with Mixtecs who work harder or at lower wages, while in other cases, Mixtecs are moving into jobs left vacant by other farm workers who have moved up the job hierarchy. Evidence that Mixtecs compete for the same labor market as mestizo workers, at least for the least skilled field labor employment, and that they work for lower wages, suggests an inevitable process of wage depression over time. The following sections describe a variety of ways this competition between Mixtecs and mestizo Mexican workers is occurring in the California farm labor market.

Displacement and Disciplining the Work Force

Several incidents show that in some cases, growers consciously use this group of extremely vulnerable workers to replace or threaten mestizo Mexican workers who put forth demands on growers, especially those who are members of unions. Mixtec workers were hired as scabs on a tomato farm near Mendota in 1990 after a mestizo labor force had gone on strike for higher piece rates. On an olive ranch in Madera county, indigenous workers from both Oaxaca and Guatemala were also brought in as strikebreakers.[15]

In a case of a citrus farm in Ventura county, the grower purposely pitted crews of Mixtec and mestizo workers against each other by threatening to fire the mestizo crew if they did not pick the same number of bins of tomatos per day as the Mixtec crews. The grower then threatened to fire the mestizo workers if they did not increase their work pace to equal the Mixtecs. On a ranch in Madera County, a grower frankly admitted his purpose in hiring Mixtecs, which was to get all his workers moving faster. He had previously been using crews from two farm labor contractors, but had become dissatisfied with their productivity. He brought in a third contractor who employed Mixtecs, and then used the new crew to set the pace of work for the other crew, and remind them that they could be replaced.[16]

These examples show that there are some instances of employers who use conscious management practices to pit Mixtec and mestizo workers against each other within their firms. In two years of field work however, we found that in general, the incorporation of Mixtecs is simply part of the everyday operation of a labor market characterized by extreme seasonality, high turnover, informality, migrancy, uncertainty, lack of enforcement of labor laws, and labor surplus.

As growers learn about a specific work force, they develop a preference for it and try to assure continued access to it. This developed preference for particular work forces has been a constant feature of the ethnic succession cycle in California farm labor history. In practice, the development of a preference for Mixtec workers among farmers leads them to replace their previous work force with Mixtecs. The following example illustrates the way in which displacement of other workers is occurring.

Buddy Edwards[17] has been farming grapes in Fresno County since 1974. He farms 27 acres and earns about $40,000 a year in net revenues from his raisin grape farm. Buddy had tremendous problems finding satisfactory labor before tapping into a network of Mixtec migrants from the town of San Miguel Cuevas. When he first bought his property in the mid-1970s, he recruited labor simply by putting up a sign in front of his property when he needed labor. This system didn't work, because no "local" (Mexican American) people would take the work, and those he did hire didn't speak English and were not steady workers. In 1978, he hired a farm labor contractor, whom he paid a 35% overhead. He was dissatisfied with the contractor, complaining that the overhead was high and even then the trays of raisins were not full. That same year, a couple workers from San Miguel Cuevas in Oaxaca worked for him, hired by the farm labor contractor.

In 1980 Buddy hired a mestizo *mayordomo* named Rodolfo, who could speak some English. Rodolfo not only serves as a supervisor, but also recruits and manages labor, performing all the functions of a labor contractor except the payroll, taxes, and other government paper work. He is not legally designated a farm labor contractor because the growers he works for are responsible for the payroll and taxes. Buddy pays Rodolfo a piece rate of two cents on every tray the workers pick, and this adds a 13% overhead to Buddy's harvesting costs.[18]

Rodolfo also supplies his work crew for a group of Buddy's neighbors under the same arrangement, who each pay Buddy a fee to defray the costs of housing the workers on his property.

When Buddy first hired him, Rodolfo recruited other people from his home town in the Mexican state of Michoacan. However, field labor was already a poor option for many of his fellow villagers, since most of them could find work as tractor drivers, in year-round jobs in nurseries, and in cities. Rodolfo therefore had to look for other sources of labor.

The two workers from San Miguel Cuevas who had worked for Buddy via his previous FLC showed up at the farm to ask for work during Rudolfo's first season, and were hired and integrated into Rudolfo's crew. Rudolfo and Buddy were very satisfied with their work and asked them to bring in more workers. In 1984, 25 people from San Miguel Cuevas came to work, and since 1987, when 60 Cuevanos worked for Buddy, Buddy's workforce has been almost exclusively from San Miguel Cuevas. As his work force has increased, Buddy has been able to add more farmers to his group. One of the other farmers in the group commented, "others would jump at the chance to be a part of our group and work with Rudolfo and his crew. We have a good thing going here". This year 110 workers, almost exclusively from San Miguel Cuevas, came for the grape harvest with Buddy and his neighbors.

The story so far looks as if the Oaxacans to a large extent simply moved into jobs that the Michoacanos from Rudolfo's village no longer wanted, as the latter found better jobs. But there are some indicators that displacement was also occurring. Buddy's neighbor had a crew of mestizo Mexicans working in his grape field and complained that they weren't working hard enough. According to this grower, the mestizos, who were long-term immigrants, were only willing to work 8 hours a day, even during the grape harvest. Moreover, each mestizo worker harvested only one row every day, each worker on Buddy's crew could do two rows in one day. So the neighbor fired his crew of mestizos and borrowed a crew of Oaxacans from Buddy in order to get his crop of raisins harvested in time. He later hired other workers from San Miguel Cuevas who he contacted through Buddy's workers. Indirectly, the Oaxacans have set the pace of work for the group of farmers that Buddy is in contact with, and this has driven some of the mestizos out of the market.

This general process was quite common. Another larger farmer in the same area, John Stillerman, had worked out a similar scheme of providing housing for a group of workers from one town. Since Stillerman farmed several hundred acres, he didn't need to make arrangements with other farmers to secure a work force. Again, his work force changed over the last ten years from one dominated by mestizo Mexicans to one composed entirely of Mixtecs from one town in Oaxaca. Tapping into this village network did not assure the return of *all* the same workers year after year. But the bulk of them do return and the ranks are renewed by the entry of more people from the same town.

Stillerman emphasized that having a reliable workforce who will go the extra mile is important in the harvest of pershable crops, in his case the delicate raisin grape crop. Raisin grapes are picked and left to dry on trays in the field . The crop will be ruined if rained upon, so growers need to have all the trays rolled up quickly to keep when a storm threatens. As Stillerman expressed it:

> This labor camp has paid for itself several times over because when I need to get my trays rolled, my workers will work until it's done. The Oaxacans are very hard workers. The workers I had before [from Michoacan] would come in at 7:30 and at 2:30 or 3:00 would tell me it's time to go home. We take our guys out at sunup. At 5:00 p.m. we ask them if they want to go home, and they say, just a little bit more By nightfall, they're ready to go home.

Finally, the survey specifically investigated the degree of labor market segmentation in the farm jobs where Mixtecs were employed. In some crops and activites, Mixtecs seemed to be the main work force, for example the Oregon strawberry harvest a job that lasts less than one month per year. Here, it seemed likely that the entry of Mixtecs had little impact on other workers, who had left these jobs voluntarily as they found better jobs of longer duration. In general, the Mixtecs worked in crews that also contained mestizo Mexican workers. Only 29 percent of the Mixtecs interviewed worked in crews composed only of Mixtecs, and no crop in California has become their exclusive domain. This indicates that mestizos and Mixtecs do compete for the same jobs, and to the extent that Mixtecs are willing to work harder or for lower wages, their entry into the labor market inevitably puts downward pressure on the wages of other farm workers.

Conclusions

After a period of significant improvement in the living and working conditions of farm workers in California from the end of the Bracero Program in 1965 to 1980, the destabilization and worsening conditions in the farm labor market over the last ten years are particularly noteworthy. The tremendous success of the United Farm Workers Union in the 1960s and 1970s in passing protective labor legislation, lobbying for social programs, and creating a political culture which gave voice to Chicanos and Mexicanos in rural California was not translated into permanent improvements in the farm labor market itself. In the current era, labor standards violations are commonplace, especially among new, vulnerable groups such as the Mixtecs. Most of the costs of seasonality, such as high job search costs, uncertainty, and seasonal unemployment, are borne by workers. Labor management practices prevail that make no attempt to minimize the costs of seasonality, because from the growers' perspective, labor can be hired and fired as easily as turning on and off a tap of water.

Decreasing wages and increasing seasonality have their roots in both economic change at the macro level and local dynamics. At the macro level, the economic integration between Mexico and the U.S. has both propelled unprecedented waves of new U.S.-bound Mexican migration and attracted United States agricultural capital to Mexico, which has become a chief competitor of California produce over the last ten years. These processes have undermined the bargaining position of workers vis-á-vis employers in the farm labor market, by creating a situation of labor surplus at the same time that pressures to reduce costs are increasing.

At the micro-level, the farm labor force is becoming increasingly heterogeneous and fragmented. Fine-tuned hierarchies within the Latino farm labor force are being created based on ethnicity, legal status, the differing collective migration histories of specific migrant networks, as well as the traditional dicotomy between U.S.-born and immigrant Mexicans. These differences within the Hispanic labor pool are often not well understood by growers or policy makers, but they are very meaningful within the farm labor community. The consequences of these fine-grained divisions is that old ties among farm workers no longer are functional. and the unifying power of the social movement led by the United Farm Workers Union has been undermined.

The case of the Mixtec migrants is particularly revealing, because Mixtecs were brought into the migration stream to the U.S. precisely by the development of vegetable production for export to the U.S. in northwest Mexico. They are one of the newest groups in California farm work today, are concentrated in the worst jobs in agriculture and receive levels of income significantly below the poverty line. Over one third of the workers interviewed received less than the minimum hourly wage of $4.25 for farm work in 1990. In addition, the ethnographic evidence suggests that growers' access to this new group of migrants leads to wage depression and higher unemployment for longer-term mestizo immigrant workers as growers develop a preference for Mixtecs in order to keep their harvesting costs down.

The entry of new, ethnically differentiated migrant groups only exacerbates the negative effects of changes in the overall macro-economic context of the farm labor market. The ability of growers to substitute lower cost workers speeds up the process of labor market destabilization and allows growers to demonstrate to all workers the decline in their bargaining power. The fragmentation of the farm labor force makes collective response to changing conditions much more difficult by pitting different groups of workers against each other and fueling the flames of ethnic antagonism.

In many ways, the cycle of ethnic replacement described in this study resembles those that have characterized the last one hundred years of farm labor relations in California agriculture. But there are also significant differences in the latest cycle of poverty. These are important both in understanding why the United Farm Workers movement could not consolidate its gains and what direction social policy can look in finding new ways to ameliorate poverty among farm workers. In previous eras, growers' influence over the political system largely accounted for the continual undermining of the labor market, through their ability to shape immigration policy and recruit new worker groups, through their success in keeping agricultural workers unprotected under national labor legislation, and through their control over local police who often repressed worker mobilizations in rural California. This political hegemony of growers has been and continues to be weakened, although only slowly.

The stark distributional battle between growers and farm workers is now overlaid with an increasingly complicated tapestry of issues. The deepening long-term structural links between rural California and rural Mexico, both within communities of workers and in firms operating on both sides of the border, present challenges to traditional strategies to promote the welfare of immigrant workers.

Historically, growers in California had a monopoly position in the production of fresh fruits and vegetables for the U. S. market. In the past, industry-wide collective bargaining could conceivably have raised wages for farm workers (with only minor impacts on U.S. consumers) because California growers faced little competition. This is no longer the case. Competition from Mexico, other regions in the U.S., and other developing countries such as Chile, threatens California's market share and has led to cost-cutting pressures on California farms.

In addition, long-term, embedded patterns of migration between rural Mexico and rural California, and the development of transnational communities now blur the distinction between U.S. and Mexican workers. Policies and strategies designed to separate domestic workers and help them at the expense of transnational workers are not sensible and can create divisions and factions among the farm labor force.

The current ethnic replacement cycle thus has a new twist. While the UFW was in fact tremendously successful in many ways and leaves an important legacy in rural California, globalization has caught up with farm labor. The internationalization of production and the on-going integration of the U.S. and Mexico foreshadows the need for both national and bi-national strategies to alleviate poverty among California farm workers.

The Mixtecs, like other foreign groups before them, have organized collective self-defense strategies (see Zabin et al. 1993; Kearney 1986; Nagengast and Kearney 1991). The Mixtec migrant associations are among the few active grassroots farm worker organizations in California today. They are built on ethnic identity, and address the plurality of problems that Mixtecs experience in their transnational voyages. From promoting small-scale community development projects in their home villages in Oaxaca, to pressing nonpayment of wage claims in California, the Mixtec leaders have combined innovative approaches to build strong binational grassroots organizations. Their visibility in the border areas has focused the attention of both U.S. government agencies and the Mexican government on the problems of Mexican migrant workers in the United States.

So far, their organizations have had little impact on conditions in the farm labor market, but there are stirrings of change. In late 1993 they signed an accord with the United Farm Workers to collaborate on activities of common interest. In addition, the federation of Oaxacan organizations throughout the state of California (the Frente Zapoteco Mixteco), has also united with the Baja California local branch of CIOAC, an agricultural workers and campesino organization in Mexico. The Mixtecs' binational organizing efforts represent a creative response to their transnational world, and will be an important piece of any renewed effort to improve the conditions of those whose hard work and sweat supply us with our fresh fruits and vegetables.

Notes

I would like to acknowledge Anna Garcia for invaluable help with field work and David Runsten for many hours of discussion of the ideas presented here.

1. It is important to note that this took place during a period in which the official minimum wage jumped from $3.35 an hour to $4.25.
2. In contrast with this pattern, the growth of Teamsters Local 890 (Salinas) is an important exception. At present their contract with Dole Fresh Vegetables Inc., a division of Dole Food Co., provides good wages, medical and dental insurance, and holiday and vacation pay for approximately 4,500 agricultural workers. This contract has been in effect for more than twenty years and is the largest union contract in U.S. agriculture.
3. The internal problems of the union and the changing state and national political environment should not be given short shrift. Majka and Majka (1992) provide an excellent analysis of the union's internal crisis in the late 1970s, which was due to the inability of the union leadership to successfully institutionalize the negotiation and management of contracts. Like for many other social movements, the transition from a protest movement to the institutionalization of change proved difficult (Majka and Majka 1992).
4. See Massey and Durand, 1992 for a discussion of the problems in estimating the number of undocumented Mexican migrants in the United States.
5. In 1986 the U.S. government passed the Immigration Reform and Control Act, commonly known as the Simpson-Rodino law or IRCA. The act had two major provisions: the employers sanctions provisions, which made it illegal for employers to knowingly hire undocumented workers, and the legalization program, which allowed some undocumented workers already integrated into the U.S. labor market to obtain legal status.
6. It also provided growers with the ability to document more workers if and when labor shortages arose, through the Replenishment Agricultural Workers or RAW program. Under the RAW provisions, if and when the program is instituted, replacement agricultural workers would be obligated to work at least 90 days in agriculture in order to retain their legal right to work in this country. The contingent nature of this program, as well as its restrictions on labor rights for future immigrant farm workers continues to generate enormous political controversy, and will be the focal point for much of the political struggles in the next several years.
7. Estimates of the size of the farm labor force are controversial. For a discussion of alternative measures, see Martin, 1989.

8. Anna Garcia, field notes, 1991.
9. Twenty-eight percent of the Mixtecs have come to the United States since 1986, when the Immigration Reform and Control Act (IRCA) was passed. This suggests that IRCA did not provide a significant deterrent for Mixtec migrants, who continued to enter the country illegally. This finding supports those of other researchers who have shown that IRCA has not been a deterrent to undocumented migration to the United States (Massey and Donato, Cornelius).
10. Detailed information was collected on the hourly wage, the hours worked per day and week, the gross and net weekly wages, benefits, the workers' transport and housing expenses, and similar data. If the job was paid on a piece rate basis, the worker was asked both the rate of pay and the volume that he/she produced per day, so that an hourly equivalent wage could be calculated from the piece rate data. For the job in which the Mixtec was working at the time of the interview, information was collected as well on the employer, the composition of the crew, how the worker found the job, and other relevant data.
11. There were no comparable *average* wage figures from the EDD survey.
12. There are several problems with this data. First they are probably biased upwards, since only those employers who comply with payroll tax laws report. Second, all workers employed by farm labor contractors are aggregated under a separate SIC code rather than reported by crop. Finally, the widespread use of fraudulent social security numbers, including the use of one number by two or more workers, makes calculations of hourly wage rates difficult to interpret.
13. The length of work seasons is only partially determined by specific crop production schedules. To a certain extent, how long each worker works is also determined by management decisions. The Cooperative Extension Service has a long history of encouraging farmers to manage their production in order to maximize the work season for their workers, thus nurturing a skilled, experienced and stable work force. However, the current incentives facing farmers are such that labor can be viewed as a variable cost of production that can be hired and fired without cost. Workers thus bear the full costs of job search and short-term unemployment, and very few farmers try to minimize these costs of seasonality.
14. Some recent econometric analyses have made a much more successful attempt to assess the impact of immigration on native-born workers by relating internal migration patterns of U.S. minority workers to international migration flows, concluding that once out-migration of African Americans is controlled for, the negative effects of immigration are much greater (Ellis, 1992).
15. Personal communication, Luis Magana, CIRS, and Roy Mendoza, Union Independiente de Trabajadores Agricolas. In both cases, the workers who were brought in as strike breakers did not know there was a labor dispute on the farm, even though under the law the employer is required to inform the newly recruited workers. Union responses have alternately supported indigenous workers and reflected ethnic antagonism. In the case of the olive farm mentioned above, Luis Magana, reported:

> [A UFW organizer] went into a field where strikebreakers were working and upon leaving made the comment, perhaps to blame someone else for his lack of ability as an organizer, that the people working there were all *Oaxaquitas* [a derogatory word for Oaxacans]. We began to really wonder whether or not this was true. Subsequently, our compañero Filemén López (from one of the Mixtec self-help groups) went out to this farm to see whether they were all Oaxacans and he told me that it wasn't true, that there were just two or three Oaxacans (the rest were Guatemalans). This is how a scapegoat is sometimes sought for

the organizer's inability to organize. (cited in Zabin, 1993).
16. Personal communication, David Runsten.
17. Real names were changed to protect the privacy of those interviewed.
18. The workers are paid 15 cents a tray, so the cost of the mayordomo is 2/15 or 13%.

References

Alvarado, Andrew, Gary Riley and Herbert Mason (1990). "Agricultural Workers in Central California in 1989," Final Research Report for California EED Contract No. M90035.

Bach, Robert (1984). "Mexican Workers in the United States." *Mondes en Developpement.* 11:43.

Bean, Frank, B. Lindsay Lowell, and Lowell Taylor (1988). "Undocumented Mexican Immigrants and the Earnings of Other Workers in the United States." *Demography,* 25, pp.35-52.

Borjas, George (1990). *Friend or Stranger: The Impact of Immigrants on the U.S. Economy.* New York: Basic Books.

California Institute for Rural Studies (1990). "Too Many Farm Workers in California? The Evidence from Wage Trends." Davis: CIRS.

Cardenas Montaño, Macrina (1991). Trabajadores Mixtecos en Madera County California. Reporte Preliminar, October.

Cook, Roberta, and Ricardo Amon (1988). "Competition in the Fresh Vegetable Industry." In Kirby Moulton et al., eds. *Competitiveness at Home and Abroad.* Davis: University of California Agricultural Issues Center.

Cornelius, Wayne A. (1989). "The U.S. Demand for Mexican Labor." In W. A. Cornelius and Jorge A. Bustamante, eds., *Mexican Migration to the United States: Origins, Consequences, and Policy Options.* La Jolla: Center for U.S.-Mexican Studies, University of California, San Diego, for the Bilateral Commission on the Future of United States-Mexican Relations.

Cornelius, Wayne A. (1992). "From Sojourners to Settlers: The Changing Profile of Mexican Immigration to the United States." In Jorge A. Bustamante, Clark W. Reynolds, and Raúl A. Hinojosa Ojeda, eds., *U.S.-Mexico Relations: Labor Market Interdependence.* Stanford, CA: Stanford University Press.

Cruz Takash, Paola and Joaquin Avila (1988). "Latino Political Participation in Rural California" *California Institute for Rural Studies Working Paper* No. 8.

Donato, Katherine, Jorge Durand, and Douglas Massey (1992). "Stemming the Tide? Assessing the Deterrent Effects of the Immigration Reform and Control Act." *Demography,* 29:2, pp. 139–57.

Fisher, Lloyd (1953). *The Harvest Labor Market in California.* Cambridge, MA: Harvard University Press.

Greenwood, Michael, and John M. McDowell (1990). *The Labor Market Consequences of U.S. Immigration: A Survey.* Boulder: Center for Economic Analysis, University of Colorado.

Jenkins, Craig (1985). *The Politics of Insurgency: The Farm Worker Movement in the 1960s.* New York: Columbia University Press.

Jones, Lamar (1970). "Labor and Management in California Agriculture, 1864–1964." *Labor History,* vol. 11, pp. 23–40.

Kearney, Michael (1986a). "Integration of the Mixteca and the Western U.S.-Mexican Border Region via Migratory Wage Labor." In Ina Rosenthal Urey, ed., *Regional*

Impacts of U.S.-Mexican Relations. Monograph Series No. 16. La Jolla: Center for U.S.-Mexican Studies, University of California, San Diego.

Levy, Jacques (1975). *Cesar Chavez: Autobiography of La Causa.* New York: Lawrence Hill and Company.

Lloyd, Jack, Philip Martin, and John Mamer (1988). "The Ventura Citrus Labor Market." *Giannini Information Series No. 88–1,* University of California, Berkeley.

Majka, Linda and Theo Majka (1982). *Farmworkers, Agribusiness, and the State.* Philadelphia: Temple University Press.

Martin, Philip (1989). "The California Farm Labor Market," *Working Group on Farm Labor and Rural Poverty Working Paper #4.*

Massey, Douglas, Rafael Alarcon, Jorge Durand, and Humberto Gonzalez (1987). *Return to Aztlan: The Social Process of International Migration from Western Mexico.* Berkeley: University of California Press.

McWilliams, Carey (1939). *Factories in the Field.* Boston: Little, Brown, and Co.

Mines, Richard and Ricardo Anzaldua (1982). *New Migrants Vs. Old Migrants: Alternative Labor Market Structures in the California Citrus Industry.* San Diego: Center for U.S.-Mexican Studies, University of California.

Nagengast, Carole and Michael Kearney (1990). "Mixtec Identity: Social Identitiy, Political Consciousness and Political Actitivism." *Latin American Research Review,* vol. 25, no. 2.

Runsten, David and Carol Zabin (1989). "Oaxacan Migrants in California Agriculture: A New Cycle of Poverty." Grant proposal for the Aspen Foundation Rural Economic Policy Program.

Runsten, David and Philip Leveen (1981). *Mechanization and Mexican Labor in California Agriculture.* San Diego: Center for U.S. Mexican Studies, University of California.

Runsten, David (1990). "Wage Trends in California Agriculture." California Institute for Rural Studies, mimeo.

Runsten, David (1991). "Some Potential Impacts of a U.S.-Mexico Free Trade Agreement on Agricultural Labor." *Rural California Report,* vol. 3, no. 1.

Runsten, David and Michael Kearney (forthcoming). *A Survey of Mixtec Village Networks in California.* Davis: California Institute for Rural Studies.

Runsten, David and Linda Wilcox (1992). "Demand for Labor, Wages, and Productivity in Mexican Fruits and Vegetables." Paper presented at the Latin American Studies Association Meetings, Los Angeles.

Varese, Stefano (1985). "Cultural Development in Ethnic Groups: Anthropological Explorations in Education." *Social Sciences of Education,* vol. 37, no. 2. UNESCO.

Varese, Stefano (1986). "Movimientos y Organizaciones Indigenas de Mexico: Balance y Perspectivas." Mimeo.

Warman, Arturo (1984). "Desarrollo Rural en areas indigenas:reflexiones a partir de la experiencia Mexicana." *Anuario Indigenista ,* vol. 44. Instituto Interamericana Indigenista.

Villarejo, Don (1989). "Farm Restructuring and Employment in California Agriculture." *Working Group on Farm Labor and Rural Poverty Working Paper #1,* California Institute for Rural Studies, Davis, CA.

Wells, Miriam and Martha West (1988). "Regulation of the Farm Labor Market: An Assessment of Farm Worker Protections Under California's Agricultural Labor Relations Act." *Working Group on Rural Poverty Working Paper 5,* California Institute for Rural Studies, Davis, CA.

Wright, Angus (1991). *The Death of Ramon Guttierrez*. Austin: University of Texas Press.

Yunez, Antonio and Ramon Blanno (1990). "Mexican Foreign Trade of Agricultural and Livestock Products: Tendencies and Impacts of Alternative Policies." Commission for the Study of International Migration and Cooperative Economic Development, *Working Paper No. 48.*

Zabin, Carol (1992). "Mixtec Migrant Farmworkers in California Agriculture: A Dialogue Among Mixtec Leaders, Researchers, and Farm Labor Advocates." Working Group on Farm Labor and Rural Poverty Working Paper No. 9. Davis: California Institute for Rural Studies. (Issued in Spanish as: Migracion Oaxaquena a los Campos Agricolas de California: Un Dialogo. Current Issues Brief No. 2. La Jolla: Center for U.S.-Mexican Studies, University of California, San Diego.)

Zabin, Carol and Grace Oseki (1990). "Oregon Farm Labor Picture, Summer 1990." *Rural California Report*, 2:4, pp.4–5.

Zabin, Carol and Sally Hughes (1995). "Economic Integration and Migration." *International Migration Review,* vol. 29, no. 2.

Zabin, Carol, Michael Kearney, Anna Garcia, and David Runsten (1993). *Mixtec Migrants in California Agriculture: A New Cycle of Poverty.* Davis, CA.: California Institute of Rural Studies.

Contributors

Jyaphia Christos-Rodgers is a doctoral student in Urban Studies at the University of New Orleans. Her research interests are urban community mobilization, race and gender, and environmental sociology. Her life experience includes years as a community organizer and as a resident of an intentional community. She is the mother to one and a friend to many children.

Corey Dolgon recently completed his Ph. D. in American Culture at the University of Michigan. He is now teaches at the Friends World Program of Long Island University.

Laura Dresser recently completed her Ph. D. in economics and social work at the University of Michigan. She now teaches economics in Boston.

Michael Kline is a doctoral candidate in the Program in American Culture at the University of Michigan. He teaches sociology at Lehigh University.

Christopher Mele teaches urban sociology at the University of North Carolina at Wilmington. His additional work on the East Village appears in Janet Abu-Lughod, et al., *From Urban Village to East Village: The Battle for New York's Lower East Side* (Blackwell). His current research interest is the experiences of living in the south for African-Americans who migrate from northern cities.

Talmadge Wright, assistant professor of sociology at Loyola University Chicago has conducted ethnographic research with marginalized homeless encampments in Orange County, California, and Chicago, Illinois. Research interests include: (1) the relationship of redevelopment to homelessness; (2) collective empowerment and social movements of the very poor; (3) mass media, social reproduction, and popular culture; and (4) social theories of urban space. He is currently working on a book entitled, "Out of Place: Homeless Mobilization, SubCities and Contested Landscapes," which examines the development of homeless collective empowerment in Chicago and San Jose, and the relationship between homeless resistance and city redevelopment policies.

Alma H. Young is a professor of urban and public affairs at the University of New Orleans. Her current research interests are the political economy of urban development, race, gender, and ethnicity in the urban environment, and the impacts of social policy on children and youth. She is president of Louisiana's advocacy agency on behalf of children, Agenda for Children.

Carol Zabin is a visiting assistant professor in the Department of Urban Planning at UCLA's School for Public Policy and Social Research. She received a Ph. D. in economics from the University of California, Berkeley, with research concentrations in economic development and labor issues. She has carried out research on immigrant labor markets in the United States, rural development in Mexico, U.S.-Mexican economic integration, and Mexican and Salvadorean migration to the United States.